W9-CLI-004

Sister Sampler
QUILTS

3 modern sampler quilts with paired sister blocks

AnneMarie Chany

Fons&Porter
CINCINNATI, OHIO

Table of Contents

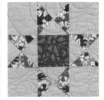

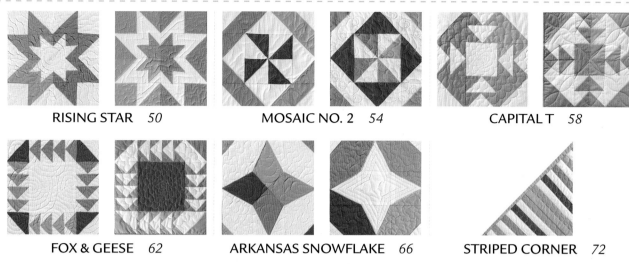

CHAPTER 3 ◆ BONFIRE SAMPLER ◆ 82

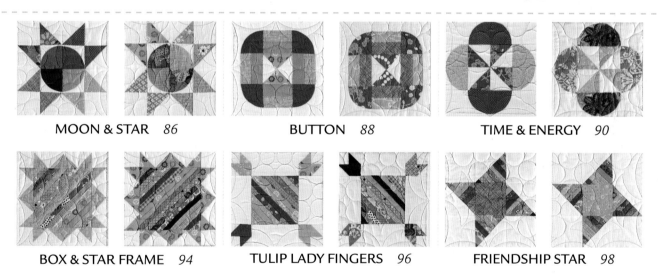

CHAPTER 4 ◆ TUTORIALS ◆ 106

INTRODUCTION

Sampler quilts have a wonderful appeal, both for quilt makers and for those who admire them. Why? Because sampler quilts are exciting to look at!

Sampler quilts have been popular for more than one hundred years. Traditionally, every block within a sampler is different, so each time you look at one of these quilts, you're sure to notice something new.

And talk about fun to work on! Instead of making forty of the same block, samplers offer variety. Each block gives you a chance to try new skills or work on improving existing ones.

I enjoy taking the idea of the traditional sampler quilt and updating it to make it modern. Modern quilts today, in 2015, are known for the use of bold colors and prints, high contrast, graphic areas of solid color, minimalism, expansive negative space and alternate grid work. I love using these elements to create new arrangements of blocks while still giving a nod to the past.

The three sampler layouts in this book are designed to feature "sisters." Sister blocks are two of the same block within a quilt that make a visually interesting design when they are arranged within the sampler setting.

In the **SISTERS' TEN SAMPLER** and **BONFIRE SAMPLER**, it's up to you if you want to make the two blocks exactly the same (identical twins) or use different fabrics for the two blocks (sisters). In the **VICE VERSA SAMPLER**, the sister blocks are made together with the second block being the inverse of the first.

I hope that making sampler quilt blocks as sisters (in pairs) allows you some freedom to play with color. Each version of a block allows you to see the results of different fabric combinations. You learn about color and value by making decisions on where to place each fabric, and with each block, you grow a little as a quilter.

The blocks in *Sister Sampler Quilts* are skill building. To help explain the basics, Chapter 4 is dedicated entirely to tutorials on the skill-building techniques. Some are great quilting classics, like Half-Square Triangles and Flying Geese. Others push you to try something new with curve or string blocks. It's up to you which blocks you choose to put in your versions of these samplers. I encourage you to make them your own.

These three sampler quilts bring traditional skill building and precision piecing practices into the modern quilt era with some fun and funky layouts. Break out of the grid and add some excitement to your sampler!

Getting Started

TOOLS

Here is a basic list of quilting tools that can be helpful when making the quilts in this book. Not all of them are necessary for every person, but I've found that having the right tools alleviates a lot of frustration.

- Sewing machine
- Sewing machine needles
- ¼" (6mm) piecing foot (optional but extremely helpful with accuracy)
- Walking foot (for straight-line quilting)
- Darning foot (for free-motion quilting)
- Thread (typically cotton thread when sewing with quilting cottons)
- Self-healing cutting mat
- Rotary cutter
- Acrylic ruler (6" × 24" [15.2cm × 61cm] or 3" × 18" [7.6cm × 45.7cm] rulers are commonly used for most cutting. A square ruler in your chosen block size, such as 9½" [24.1cm] or 12½" [31.8cm] is helpful when squaring up blocks and smaller block components like half-square triangles, but these are optional.)
- Scissors
- Seam ripper
- Iron and ironing board
- Pins
- Safety pins
- Fabric marker (I prefer Frixion pens that disappear when heat is applied)
- Paper for string blocks (I like notebook paper. It's thinner than computer paper and perforates easily.)
- Double-sided tape (optional for string blocks)

CHOOSE YOUR OWN ADVENTURE . . . SAMPLER STYLE

To me, quilting is fun and about interpretation. I'm providing you with these patterns as a guide. Feel free to adapt them to your liking. After all, *you* are the person who will keep the quilt or gift it to a loved one.

SUBSTITUTE ANY BLOCK: This book provides instructions for twenty-five quilt blocks and three sampler quilt layouts. The samples I've made represent only three possible quilts that can be made from these blocks. Feel free to "choose your own adventure" and create a unique sampler from any combination of these blocks.

SISTER BLOCKS WORK IN PAIRS: Remember that the samplers in this book contain sister blocks. Sister blocks are usually two of the same block made with different color fabrics. The sampler layouts always contain pairs of the same block in their settings, but it's up to you whether you want to make two of each block. If not, you'll need more individual blocks to make up the total number needed for each quilt layout.

SIZE MATTERS: All quilt block instructions are provided in two sizes: 9" (22.9cm) and 12" (30.5cm) finished blocks. This allows you make a quilt sized to your liking. It may be helpful to flag the instructions for the size you are making as you work through the book. I

Cutting supplies: Mat, rulers, rotary cutter and scissors.

Sewing supplies: Machine feet and needles, pins, binding clips, marking tools, seam ripper and thread.

like to use sticky notes to cover the cutting instructions I don't need so I don't get confused.

CHOOSING FABRICS

For the three sampler quilts in this book, I worked with three different methods of fabric selection. In the **SISTERS' TEN SAMPLER**, the fabrics I chose were entirely from one fabric collection (Lucky Penny by Alison Glass for Andover). In the **VICE VERSA SAMPLER**, I worked only with solid fabrics. Lastly, in the **BONFIRE SAMPLER**, I chose fabrics from various fabric collections and manufacturers, as well as a few solids to create a scrappier look.

Take a look at the quilt you want to make and decide what method of selecting fabric works for you.

FIND YOUR COLOR PALETTE: I would suggest finding a color palette that really wows you. Design-seeds.com is a great place to start, but Pinterest.com is also a great resource. Search for "color palette" on Pinterest, and you'll find lots of inspiration.

When choosing a palette, look for one that offers enough variety in color. For example, while a palette of various gray shades may be soothing in home décor, it might not produce enough contrast for these quilts. You want the blocks to pop, and your fabric selection will make that happen.

Choose a palette with several distinct colors rather than palettes with only a few colors in a similar range. You want your colors to pop, not run together across your quilt!

SOLIDS, BLENDERS OR BOTH?: After you've picked your palette, decide what kind of fabrics you want in your stack for this quilt. Solids are an easy choice, but don't think you're limited to just that! Blenders, tone-on-tone prints and tone-and-white prints can all work beautifully in these quilts. I do suggest sticking with small-scale prints, however. These quilts focus on the piecing, and large-scale prints might lose their impact when stitched into these smaller shapes.

Fabric requirements are provided as straight yardage and/or fat quarter requirements. If you'd like to add variety to your quilt, just make sure you have the appropriate total yardage of each color. You can have several fat quarters or scraps combining solids, tone-on-tones and prints within that particular color.

BEFORE YOU BEGIN

I highly recommend doing a quick test to make sure you're sewing a scant ¼" (6mm) seam before you begin piecing blocks. It will greatly improve the accuracy of your blocks and save some of your sanity! See the Scant Rant tutorial in Chapter 4 for more information.

Palette inspiration for the **VICE VERSA SAMPLER**. These colors are distinct and interesting.

A palette with colors that are too similar. These colors won't pop in a quilt.

Fabric pull for the **VICE VERSA SAMPLER** based on the inspiration palette.

Chapter 1

SISTERS' TEN SAMPLER

This quilt's theme centers around your favorite women. Be it a wife, mother, grandmother, aunt, sister or friend, we all have a woman we look up to and aspire to be like. These ten quilt blocks honor those women in the blocks' names, such as Sister's Choice and Grandmother's Frame. Quilts are a great way to commemorate these women.

Beautiful classic blocks look stunning in this modern setting. The blocks are made in two colorways for each pattern, creating pairs or sisters.

The quilt is designed in halves. Each half houses ten blocks. The sister blocks can be placed in opposing halves of the quilt to create an asymmetrical balance.

Finished sizes:	Lap—60" (152.4cm) square (9" [22.9cm] finished blocks)
	Large Twin—78" (198.1cm) square (12" [30.5cm] finished blocks)
Number of blocks:	20 (make 2 from each of 10 patterns)
Skill level:	Confident beginner—Intermediate

◄ **SISTERS'**
TEN SAMPLER,
designed and pieced by AnneMarie Chany. Quilted by Kathy Balmert.

Materials

Fabric estimates are based on yardage with 42" (106.7cm) of usable fabric.
Fat quarters are 18" × 22" (45.7cm × 55.9cm).

LAP—60" (152.4CM) SQUARE (9" [22.9CM] FINISHED BLOCKS)

9 fat quarters (for Fabrics B, C, D and E)

3 yards (2.7m) for background and sashing (Fabric A)

½ yard (0.5m) of binding fabric

3¾ yards (3.4m) for pieced backing

68" (172.7cm) square of batting

LARGE TWIN—78" (198.1CM) SQUARE (12" [30.5CM] FINISHED BLOCKS)

12 fat quarters (for Fabrics B, C, D and E)

4⅝ yards (4.2m) for background and sashing (Fabric A)

⅝ yard (0.6m) of binding fabric

4¾ yards (4.3m) for pieced backing

86" (218.4cm) square of batting

Fabric shown in project is Lucky Penny by Alison Glass for Andover Fabrics, with Quilter's Linen in Straw by Robert Kaufman for the background.

CUTTING INSTRUCTIONS FOR SASHING AND NEGATIVE SPACE

Cut large background pieces and sashing strips before you begin working through the blocks. Set these pieces aside until you have completed all blocks for the quilt.

FROM FABRIC A

For 9" (22.9cm) blocks, cut

Twelve 1½" × 9½" (3.8cm × 24.1cm) strips (A)

Two 9½" × 20½" (24.1cm × 52.1cm) rectangles (B)

Two 9½" × 30½" (24.1cm × 77.5cm) rectangles (C)

Two 9½" × 31½" (24.1cm × 80cm) rectangles (D)

Five 1½" × 59½" (3.8cm × 151.1cm) strips (E)

For 12" (30.5cm) blocks, cut

Twelve 1½" × 12½" (3.8cm × 31.8cm) strips (A)

Two 12½" × 26½" (31.8cm × 67.3cm) rectangles (B)

Two 12½" × 39½" (31.8cm × 100.3cm) rectangles (C)

Two 12½" × 40½" (31.8cm × 102.9cm) rectangles (D)

Five 1½" × 77½" (3.8cm × 196.9cm) strips (E)

PIECING EXTRA-LONG STRIPS

Note that some of the sashing strips are very long and will require cutting a few width-of-fabric strips and piecing them together to get the total strip length.

For example, to make the 1½" × 59½" (3.8cm × 151.1cm) strips, cut eight 1½" × wof (3.8cm × wof) strips and use those to make five 1½" × 59½" (3.8cm × 151.1cm) strips.

Grandmother's Frame

We're getting started with a great block called Grandmother's Frame. It has a large center square that's perfect for fussy cutting a larger print.

Grandmother's Frame Block no. 1

Grandmother's Frame Block no. 2

CUTTING INSTRUCTIONS

Fabric A is the background fabric. Fabric B–Fabric E are chosen from various fat quarters.

FUSSY CUT

To target and center a certain motif or print of quilting fabric, rather than to cut randomly. Fussy cutting is used in a lot of I-Spy quilts, where the center squares are cut to feature a novelty or pictorial object within the block. Frame blocks are a fun place to try this technique.

FOR 9" (22.9CM) BLOCKS

From Fabric A, cut
Four 3" (7.6cm) squares

Four 2" × 2⅜" (5.1cm × 6cm) rectangles

From Fabrics B and C, cut
Two 3" (7.6cm) squares

From Fabric D, cut
One 5¾" (14.6cm) square (fussy cut if desired)

From Fabric E, cut
Four 3" (7.6cm) squares

FOR 12" (30.5CM) BLOCKS

From Fabric A, cut
Four 3¾" (9.5cm) squares

Four 2½" × 3" (6.4cm × 7.6cm) rectangles

From Fabrics B and C, cut
Two 3¾" (9.5cm) squares

From Fabric D, cut
One 7½" (19.1cm) square (fussy cut if desired)

From Fabric E, cut
Four 3¾" (9.5cm) squares

PIECING INSTRUCTIONS

1 Make Half-Square Triangle (HST) units with Fabric A and Fabric E. Use the 4 Fabric A squares and the 4 Fabric E squares to make 8 total HST units. See the Half-Square Triangle tutorial in Chapter 4 for details on making HSTs and squaring up.

The HSTs should be trimmed to the following sizes:
- ▶ For 9″ (22.9cm) blocks: 2⅜″ (6cm), unfinished
- ▶ For 12″ (30.5cm) blocks: 3″ (7.6cm), unfinished

2 Make HST units with Fabric B and Fabric C. Use the 2 Fabric B squares and the 2 Fabric C squares to make 4 total HSTs.

The HSTs should be trimmed down to the following dimensions:
- ▶ For 9″ blocks: 2⅜″ (6cm), unfinished
- ▶ For 12″ blocks: 3″ (7.6cm), unfinished

3 Lay out the HST units, remaining Fabric A rectangles and Fabric D square (Figure 1).

4 Sew the HSTs and squares on the left and right sides of the Fabric D square together (Figure 2).

5 Sew the rows from step 4 to the left and right sides of the Fabric D square. Next, sew the top and bottom HSTs and squares together (Figure 3).

6 Sew the top and bottom rows to the center section to complete the block (Figure 4).

7 Make 2 blocks for the **SISTERS' TEN SAMPLER** quilt.

Figure 1

Figure 2

Figure 3

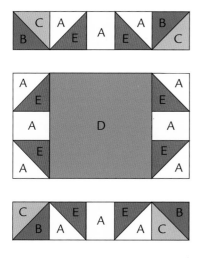

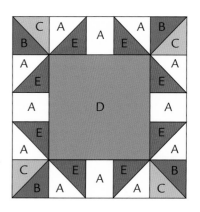

Figure 4

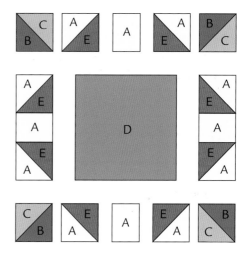

Susannah

This block has a Diamond-in-the-Square at the center and a windmill-like appearance. For a completely different look, try making Susannah with scraps. Each blade of the windmill could be a different color.

Susannah Block no. 1

Susannah Block no. 2

CUTTING INSTRUCTIONS

Fabric A is the background fabric. Fabric B–Fabric C are chosen from various fat quarters.

FOR 9" (22.9CM) BLOCKS

From Fabric A, cut
Eight 2¾" (7cm) squares

From Fabric B, cut
Eight 2¾" (7cm) squares

From Fabric C, cut
One 5" (12.7cm) square

FOR 12" (30.5CM) BLOCKS

From Fabric A, cut
Eight 3½" (8.9cm) squares

From Fabric B, cut
Eight 3½" (8.9cm) squares

From Fabric C, cut
One 6½" (16.5cm) square

PIECING

1 Make a Diamond-in-the-Square unit with Fabric B and Fabric C. Draw a diagonal line on the wrong side of 4 Fabric B squares. Layer 2 of the Fabric B squares atop the Fabric C square as shown with right sides together. Sew on the drawn lines. Trim the excess ¼" (6mm) away from the stitching and press seams toward Fabric B. Repeat these steps with the 2 remaining Fabric B squares to complete the block (Figure 1).

The Diamond-in-the-Square block should be trimmed to the following dimensions:

- ▶ For 9" (22.9cm) blocks: 5" (12.7cm), unfinished
- ▶ For 12" (30.5cm) blocks: 6½" (16.5cm), unfinished

2 Lay out the Diamond-in-the-Square unit, Fabric A squares and remaining Fabric B squares (Figure 2).

3 Sew the Fabric A and B squares on the left and right sides of the Diamond-in-the-Square center together. Next, sew the top and bottom Fabric A and B squares together (Figure 3).

4 Sew the paired rows to the left and right sides of the Diamond-in-the-Square. Sew the top and bottom rows to the center section (Figure 4).

5 Make 2 blocks for the **SISTERS' TEN SAMPLER** quilt.

Figure 1

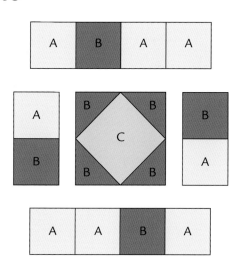

Figure 2

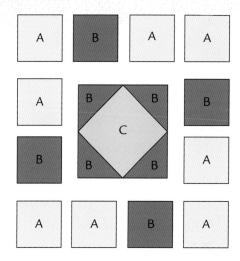

Figure 3

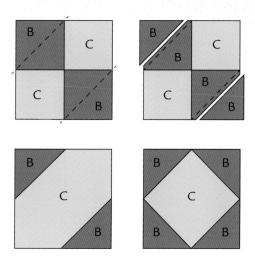

Figure 4

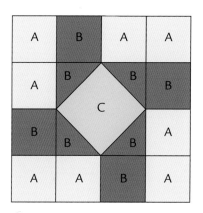

School Girl's Puzzle

This block has a unique overall shape that reminds me of a jewel. It consists of only simple Half-Square Triangles and square patches, so it's a snap to sew.

School Girl's Puzzle Block no. 1

School Girl's Puzzle Block no. 2

CUTTING INSTRUCTIONS

Fabric A is the background fabric. Fabric B–Fabric D are chosen from various fat quarters.

FOR 9" (22.9CM) BLOCKS

From Fabric A, cut
Five 3⅜" (8.6cm) squares

From Fabric B, cut
Two 3⅜" (8.6cm) squares

From Fabric C, cut
Three 3⅜" (8.6cm) squares (large)

Two 2¾" (7cm) squares

From Fabric D, cut
Four 2¾" (7cm) squares

FOR 12" (30.5CM) BLOCKS

From Fabric A, cut
Five 4⅛" (10.5cm) squares

From Fabric B, cut
Two 4⅛" (10.5cm) squares

From Fabric C, cut
Three 4⅛" (10.5cm) squares (large)

Two 3½" (8.9cm) squares

From Fabric D, cut
Four 3½" (8.9cm) squares

16

PIECING

1 Make Half-Square Triangle (HST) units with Fabric A and Fabric B. Use 2 Fabric A squares and the 2 Fabric B squares to make 4 total HST units. See the Half-Square Triangle tutorial in Chapter 4 for details on making HSTs and squaring up.

The HSTs should be trimmed to the following dimensions:
- ► For 9″ (22.9cm) blocks: 2¾″ (7cm), unfinished
- ► For 12″ (30.5cm) blocks: 3½″ (8.9cm), unfinished

2 Make HST units with Fabric A and Fabric C. Use the remaining 3 Fabric A squares and the 3 larger Fabric C squares to make 6 total HST units.

The HSTs should be trimmed to the following dimensions:
- ► For 9″ (22.9cm) blocks: 2¾″ (7cm), unfinished
- ► For 12″ (30.5cm) blocks: 3½″ (8.9cm), unfinished

3 Lay out the HST units, the remaining Fabric C squares and the Fabric D squares as shown in Figure 1.

4 Sew the units together into 4 rows (Figure 2).

5 Sew the 4 rows together to complete the block (Figure 3).

6 Make 2 blocks for the **SISTERS' TEN SAMPLER** quilt.

Figure 1

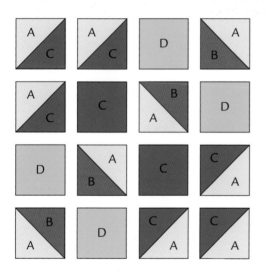

Figure 2

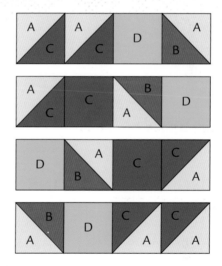

Figure 3

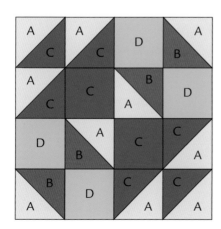

Lady of the Lake

Get ready to get your Half-Square Triangles on—it's Lady of the Lake. Twenty-one Half-Square Triangles make this block an eye-catching beauty. There's one large Half-Square Triangle in the center of this block where you can use a fabric you'd really like to feature.

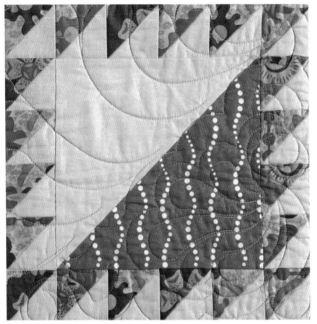

Lady of the Lake Block no. 1

Lady of the Lake Block no. 2

CUTTING INSTRUCTIONS

Fabric A is the background fabric. Fabric B and Fabric C are chosen from various fat quarters.

LARGE HSTS

To avoid excessive waste, make the large center Half-Square Triangles as a pair, then use one large HST for Block no. 1 and one for Block no. 2. Don't worry if you think they look too similar! Once the blocks are separated on opposite sides of the quilt, it won't be noticeable.

FOR 9" (22.9CM) BLOCKS

From Fabric A, cut
Ten 2⅝" (6.7cm) squares

One 7¼" (18.4cm) square (large)

From Fabric B, cut
One 7¼" (18.4cm) square

From Fabric C, cut
Ten 2⅝" (6.7cm) squares

FOR 12" (30.5CM) BLOCKS

From Fabric A, cut
Ten 3⅛" (8cm) squares

One 9¼" (23.5cm) square (large)

From Fabric B, cut
One 9¼" (23.5cm) square

From Fabric C, cut
Ten 3⅛" (8cm) squares

PIECING

1 Make a Half-Square Triangle (HST) unit with Fabric A and Fabric B. Use the large Fabric A square and the Fabric B square to make 2 total HST units. See the Half-Square Triangle tutorial in Chapter 4 for details on making HSTs and squaring up.

The HSTs should be trimmed to the following dimensions:
▸ For 9″ (22.9cm) blocks: 6½″ (16.5cm), unfinished
▸ For 12″ (30.5cm) blocks: 8½″ (21.6cm), unfinished

2 Make HST units with Fabric A and Fabric C. Use the remaining 10 Fabric A squares and the 10 Fabric C squares to make 20 total HST units.

The HSTs should be trimmed to the following dimensions:
▸ For 9″ (22.9cm) blocks: 2″ (5.1cm), unfinished
▸ For 12″ (30.5cm) blocks: 2½″ (6.4cm), unfinished

3 Lay out the HST units (Figure 1).

4 Sew together each of the 4 rows that surround the center HST. The side rows should include 4 HSTs; the top and bottom rows should include 6 HSTs (Figure 2).

5 Sew the rows on the left and right sides to the center HST (Figure 3).

6 Sew the remaining rows to the top and bottom of the center section (Figure 4) to complete the block.

7 Make 2 blocks for the **SISTERS' TEN SAMPLER** quilt.

Figure 1

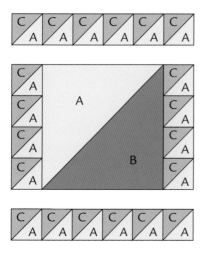

Figure 2

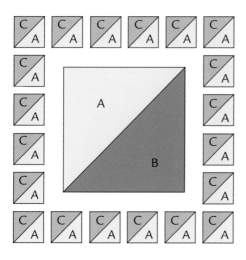

Figure 3

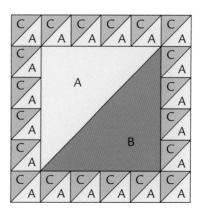

Figure 4

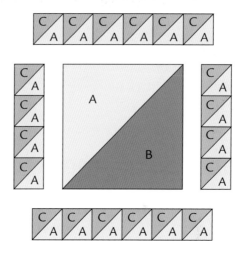

Aunt Eliza's Star

This block uses a new fundamental block: the Hourglass. Four Hourglass blocks combine with square patches to create a star for Aunt Eliza's Star.

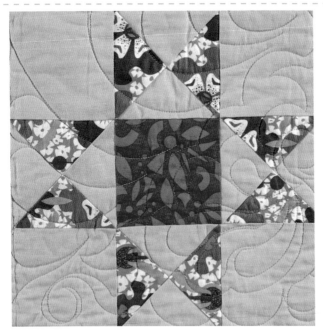

Aunt Eliza's Star Block no. 1

Aunt Eliza's Star Block no. 2

CUTTING INSTRUCTIONS

Fabric A is the background fabric. Fabric B–Fabric C are chosen from various fat quarters.

ONE- OR TWO- COLOR STARS

Notice that the example blocks for Aunt Eliza's Star are slightly different. The first block uses only one fabric in the star points. The second block uses two fabrics in those same points. Decide which look you prefer and go for it! To make star points in two colors, cut only one square from Fabric B and cut another square of the same size from a second fabric.

FOR 9" (22.9CM) BLOCKS

From Fabric A, cut
Four 3½" (8.9cm) squares

Two 4½" (11.4cm) squares (large)

From Fabric B, cut
Two 4½" (11.4cm) squares

From Fabric C, cut
One 3½" (8.9cm) square

FOR 12" (30.5CM) BLOCKS

From Fabric A, cut
Four 4½" (11.4cm) squares

Two 5½" (14cm) squares (large)

From Fabric B, cut
Two 5½" (14cm) squares

From Fabric C, cut
One 4½" (11.4cm) square

PIECING

1 Make Hourglass units with Fabric A and Fabric B. Use 2 larger Fabric A squares and the 2 Fabric B squares to make 4 Hourglass units. See the Quarter-Square Triangle (QST) tutorial in Chapter 4 for details on making QSTs, Hourglass blocks and squaring up.

The Hourglass units should be trimmed to the following dimensions:

- ▸ For 9″ (22.9cm) blocks: 3½″ (8.9cm), unfinished
- ▸ For 12″ (30.5cm) blocks: 4½″ (11.4cm), unfinished

2 Lay out the Hourglass units and the remaining Fabric A and Fabric C squares (Figure 1).

3 Sew the units together into 3 rows (Figure 2).

4 Sew the 3 rows together to complete the block (Figure 3).

5 Make 2 blocks for the **SISTERS' TEN SAMPLER** quilt.

Figure 1

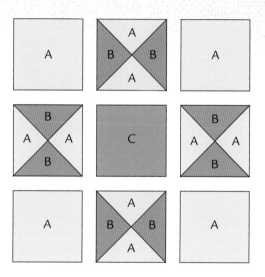

Figure 2

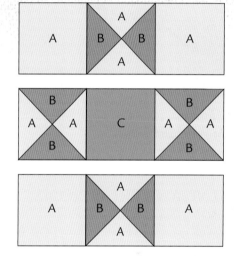

Figure 3

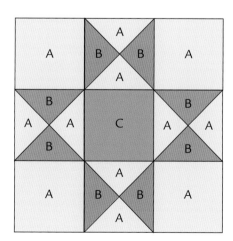

Contrary Wife

The Contrary Wife block is simple and elegant. It uses only four Half-Square Triangles and square patches in a Nine Patch setting.

Contrary Wife Block no. 1

Contrary Wife Block no. 2

CUTTING INSTRUCTIONS

Fabric A is the background fabric. Fabric B–Fabric D are chosen from various fat quarters.

FOR 9" (22.9CM) BLOCKS

From Fabric A, cut
Two 4¼" (10.8cm) squares

From Fabric B, cut
Two 4¼" (10.8cm) squares

From Fabric C, cut
Three 3½" (8.9cm) squares

From Fabric D, cut
Two 3½" (8.9cm) squares

FOR 12" (30.5CM) BLOCKS

From Fabric A, cut
Two 5¼" (13.3cm) squares

From Fabric B, cut
Two 5¼" (13.3cm) squares

From Fabric C, cut
Three 4½" (11.4cm) squares

From Fabric D, cut
Two 4½" (11.4cm) squares

PIECING

1 Make Half-Square Triangle (HST) units with Fabric A and Fabric B. Use the 2 Fabric A squares and the 2 Fabric B squares to make 4 total HST units. See the Half-Square Triangle tutorial in Chapter 4 for details on making HSTs and squaring up.

The HSTs should be trimmed to the following dimensions:
- ▶ 9″ (22.9cm) blocks: 3½″ (8.9cm), unfinished
- ▶ 12″ (30.5cm) blocks: 4½″ (11.4cm), unfinished

2 Lay out the HST units, the remaining Fabric C squares and the Fabric D squares (Figure 1).

3 Sew the units together into 3 rows (Figure 2).

4 Sew the 3 rows together to complete the block (Figure 3).

5 Make 2 blocks for the **SISTERS' TEN SAMPLER** quilt.

Figure 1

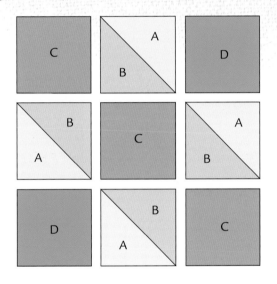

Figure 2

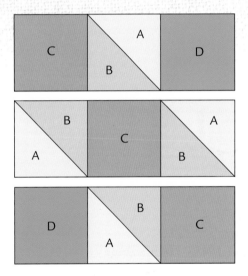

Figure 3

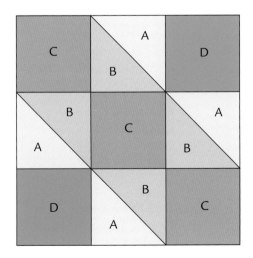

Hattie's Trick

Hattie's Trick, which is named after a quilter in my husband's family, is another simple block that plays with a combination of Half-Square Triangles and square patches. This block has been renamed for the SISTERS' TEN SAMPLER. It's also known as the Double X no. 1, but that name is neither sisterly nor exciting!

Hattie's Trick Block no. 1

Hattie's Trick Block no. 2

CUTTING INSTRUCTIONS

Fabric A is the background fabric. Fabric B–Fabric D are chosen from various fat quarters.

FOR 9" (22.9CM) BLOCKS	FOR 12" (30.5CM) BLOCKS
From Fabric A, cut	*From Fabric A, cut*
Three 4¼" (10.8cm) squares	Three 5¼" (13.3cm) squares
Two 3½" (8.9cm) squares	Two 4½" (11.4cm) squares
From Fabric B, cut	*From Fabric B, cut*
One 3½" (8.9cm) square	One 4½" (11.4cm) square
From Fabric C, cut	*From Fabric C, cut*
One 4¼" (10.8cm) square	One 5¼" (13.3cm) square
From Fabric D, cut	*From Fabric D, cut*
One 4¼" (10.8cm) square	One 5¼" (13.3cm) square
From Fabric E, cut	*From Fabric E, cut*
One 4¼" (10.8cm) square	One 5¼" (13.3cm) square

PIECING

1 Make 6 Half-Square Triangle (HST) units, pairing the 3 Fabric A squares with Fabric C, D and E respectively. See the Half-Square Triangle tutorial in Chapter 4 for details on making HSTs and squaring up.

The HSTs should be trimmed to the following dimensions:
- ▸ 9″ (22.9cm) blocks: 3½″ (8.9cm), unfinished
- ▸ 12″ (30.5cm) blocks: 4½″ (11.4cm), unfinished

2 Lay out the HST units, remaining Fabric A squares and the Fabric B square (Figure 1).

3 Sew the units together into 3 rows (Figure 2).

4 Sew the 3 rows together to complete the block (Figure 3).

5 Make 2 blocks for the **SISTERS' TEN SAMPLER** quilt.

Figure 1

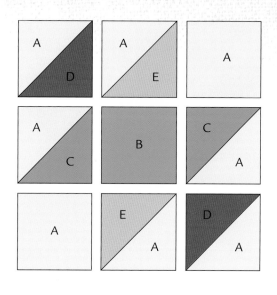

Figure 2

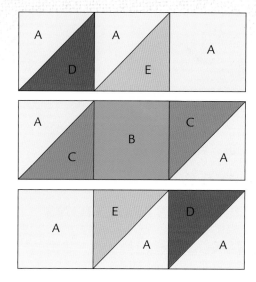

Figure 3

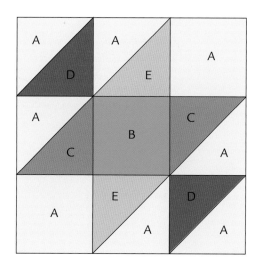

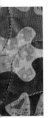

Old Maid's Puzzle

The Old Maid's Puzzle block is a very attractive design. It uses a combination of triangles in two different sizes and square patches.

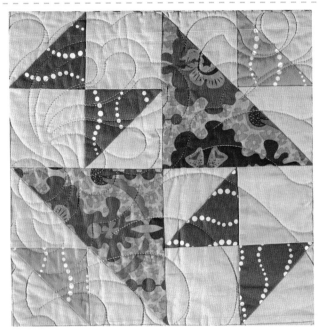

Old Maid's Puzzle Block no. 1

Old Maid's Puzzle Block no. 2

CUTTING INSTRUCTIONS

Fabric A is the background fabric. Fabric B–Fabric D are chosen from various fat quarters.

FOR 9" (22.9CM) BLOCKS

From Fabric A, cut
Three 3½" (8.9cm) squares (large)

Two 3⅛" (7.9cm) squares (medium)

Four 2¾" (7cm) squares

From Fabric B, cut
Two 3½" (8.9cm) squares

From Fabric C, cut
One 3½" (8.9cm) square

From Fabric D, cut
One 5⅜" (13.7cm) square

FOR 12" (30.5CM) BLOCKS

From Fabric A, cut
Three 4¼" (10.8cm) squares (large)

Two 3⅞" (9.8cm) squares (medium)

Four 3½" (8.9cm) squares

From Fabric B, cut
Two 4¼" (10.8cm) squares

From Fabric C, cut
One 4¼" (10.8cm) square

From Fabric D, cut
One 6⅞" (17.5cm) square

PIECING

1 Make Half-Square Triangle (HST) units using 2 of the large Fabric A squares and the 2 Fabric B squares to make 4 total HST units, then pair the remaining large Fabric A square with the Fabric C square to make 2 total HST units. See the Half-Square Triangle tutorial in Chapter 4 for details on making HSTs and squaring up.

The HSTs should be trimmed to the following dimensions:
  ▸ 9" (22.9cm) blocks: 2¾" (7cm), unfinished
  ▸ 12" (30.5cm) blocks: 3½" (8.9cm), unfinished

2 Cut the 2 medium Fabric A squares and 1 Fabric D square into triangles by cutting diagonally across the square (Figure 1).

3 Lay out the HST units, the Fabric A and Fabric D triangles and the remaining Fabric A squares (Figure 2).

4 Sew the Bow Tie four-patch blocks together (upper left quadrant and lower right quadrant). First, sew the 2 units in each row together, pairing 1 A/B HST with one A square. Then sew the 2 rows together to make the four-patch block (Figure 3).

5 Next, sew the triangle quadrants. Like the diagram in step 1 of Figure 4, place 1 Fabric A triangle on top of 1 A/C HST. Stitch across the top of the block. Press the Fabric A triangle up as in step 2. Place another Fabric A triangle along the right side of the unit from Step 2, as shown in step 3. Stitch across the right side of the unit as shown. Press the Fabric A triangle to the right as shown in step 4 (Figure 4).

As shown in step 5 (Figure 4), sew a Fabric D triangle to the unit from step 4 to complete the quadrant. Place the Fabric D triangle directly on top of the step 4 unit (not shown) and sew along the hypotenuse of the pair. Press the Fabric D triangle open as shown in step 6. Repeat for remaining triangle quadrant.

6 Now all 4 sections of the block are assembled. Lay them out and sew the units in each row together to make 2 rows (Figure 5).

7 Sew the 2 rows together to complete the block (Figure 6).

8 Make 2 blocks for the **SISTERS' TEN SAMPLER** quilt.

Figure 1

Figure 2

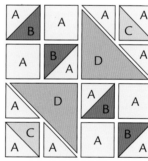

Figure 3

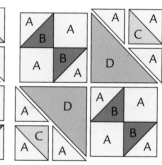

Figure 4

Figure 5

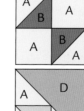

Figure 6

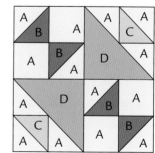

Sister's Choice

The Sister's Choice block is so simple in its construction, yet playing with five different fabrics can yield such a lovely design visually. If I had to pick my favorite quilt block, Sister's Choice would be it.

Sister's Choice Block no. 1

Sister's Choice Block no. 2

CUTTING INSTRUCTIONS

Fabric A is the background fabric. Fabric B–Fabric E are chosen from various fat quarters.

FOR 9" (22.9CM) BLOCKS

From Fabric A, cut
Four 2⅜" (6cm) squares
Four 3" (7.6cm) squares (large)

From Fabric B, cut
Four 2" × 2⅜" (5.1cm × 6cm) rectangles

From Fabric C, cut
Four 2⅜" (6cm) squares

From Fabric D, cut
Four 2" × 2⅜" (5.1cm × 6cm) rectangles

From Fabric E, cut
One 2" (5.1cm) square
Four 3" (7.6cm) squares (large)

FOR 12" (30.5CM) BLOCKS

From Fabric A, cut
Four 3" (7.6cm) squares
Four 3¾" (9.5cm) squares (large)

From Fabric B, cut
Four 2½" × 3" (6.4cm × 7.6cm) rectangles

From Fabric C, cut
Four 3" (7.6cm) squares

From Fabric D, cut
Four 2½" × 3" (6.4cm × 7.6cm) rectangles

From Fabric E, cut
One 2½" (6.4cm) square
Four 3¾" (9.5cm) squares (large)

PIECING

1 Make 8 Half-Square Triangle (HST) units, pairing the 4 large Fabric A squares with the 4 large Fabric E squares. See the Half-Square Triangle tutorial in Chapter 4 for details on making HSTs and squaring up.

The HSTs should be trimmed to the following dimensions:
- ▸ 9″ (22.9cm) blocks: 2⅜″ (6cm), unfinished
- ▸ 12″ (30.5cm) blocks: 3″ (7.6cm), unfinished

2 Lay out the HST units; remaining Fabric A, Fabric C and Fabric E squares; and Fabric B and Fabric D rectangles (Figure 1).

3 Sew the units together to make 5 rows (Figure 2).

4 Sew the 5 rows together to complete the block (Figure 3).

5 Make 2 blocks for the **SISTERS' TEN SAMPLER** quilt.

Figure 1

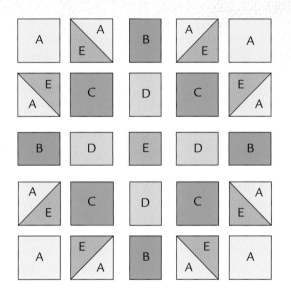

Figure 2

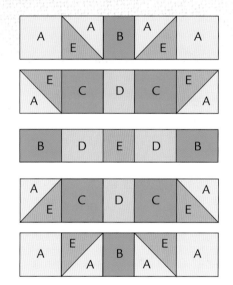

Figure 3

Aunt Lee's Frame

Frame blocks often feature a fussy-cut motif and/or a quilt dedication. Aunt Lee's Frame uses Flying Geese and some triangle piecework (similar to Old Maid's Puzzle) to frame the center square.

The second version of this block features a custom label for the sampler quilt in the 12" (30.5cm) block size. This dedicates the quilt on the front rather than the back.

Aunt Lee's Frame Block no. 1

Aunt Lee's Frame Block no. 2

CUTTING INSTRUCTIONS

Fabric A is the background fabric. Fabric B–Fabric E are chosen from various fat quarters.

FOR 9" (22.9CM) BLOCKS

From Fabric A, cut
One 5¾" (14.6cm) square (large)
Two 3⅛" (7.9cm) squares (medium)

From Fabric B, cut
Four 3⅛" (7.9cm) squares

From Fabric C, cut
Four 2" (5.1cm) squares

From Fabric D, cut
Four 1⅝" (4.1cm) squares

From Fabric E, cut
One 5" (12.7cm) square or use a 5" (12.7cm) label

FOR 12" (30.5CM) BLOCKS

From Fabric A, cut
One 7¼" (18.4cm) square (large)
Two 3⅞" (9.8cm) squares (medium)

If using a custom label, cut
Two 1¼" × 5" (3.2cm × 12.7cm) rectangles
Two 1¼" × 6½" (3.2cm × 16.5cm) rectangles

From Fabric B, cut
Four 3⅞" (9.8cm) squares

From Fabric C, cut
Four 2⅜" (6cm) squares

From Fabric D, cut
Four 2" (5.1cm) squares

From Fabric E, cut
One 6½" (16.5cm) square*

*If using a custom label, instead trim label to 5" (12.7cm) square

1 Make No-Waste Flying Geese units using Fabric A and Fabric B. Use the 1 large Fabric A square and the 4 Fabric B squares to make 4 Flying Geese units. See the No-Waste Flying Geese tutorial in Chapter 4 for details.

The Flying Geese dimensions should measure the following:

- ▸ 9" (22.9cm) blocks: 2¾" × 5" (7cm × 12.7cm), unfinished
- ▸ 12" (30.5cm) blocks: 3½" × 6½" (8.9cm × 16.5cm), unfinished

2 Cut the 2 medium Fabric A squares and the 4 Fabric C squares into triangles by cutting diagonally across the square (Figure 1).

3 **Assemble Corner Units** (Figure 2). As in step 1 of Figure 2, place 1 Fabric C triangle on top of 1 Fabric D square. Stitch across the top of the block. Press the Fabric C triangle upward as in step 2. Place another Fabric C triangle along the right side of the unit from step 2, as shown in step 3. Stitch across the right side of the unit. Press the Fabric C triangle to the right as shown in step 4.

As shown in step 5, sew a Fabric A triangle to the unit made in step 4 to complete the quadrant. Place the Fabric A triangle directly on top of the step 4 unit (not shown) and sew along the diagonal of the pair. Press the Fabric A triangle open as shown in step 6. Make 4 corner units.

4 **For custom label only in 12" (30.5cm) blocks:** Sew the 1¼" × 5" (3.2cm × 12.7cm) Fabric A rectangles to the left and right sides of the 5" (12.7cm) label. Then sew the 1¼" × 6½" (3.2cm × 16.5cm) rectangles to the top and bottom of the unit. Use this as the Fabric E square in your block (Figure 3).

5 Lay out the Flying Geese units, the corner units and the Fabric E square (Figure 4).

6 Sew the units together to make 3 rows (Figure 5).

7 Sew the 3 rows together to complete the block (Figure 6).

8 Make 2 blocks for the **SISTERS' TEN SAMPLER** quilt.

Figure 1

Figure 2

Figure 3

SISTER'S TEN
modern
BOM

with
gen X quilters

Figure 4

Figure 5

Figure 6

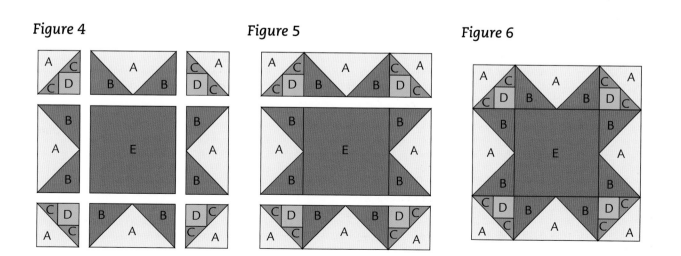

Assemble the Quilt Top

See the Cutting Instructions for Sashing and Negative Space on page 11 for cutting and labeling your sashing.

Laying out the block arrangement for a sampler quilt is incredibly fun. There are many combinations, and I encourage you to lay out the blocks in an arrangement that suits the color distribution in your blocks.

The layout I chose was based on how I found the blocks visually pleasing. You have made two of each block. Generally, the pairs of blocks are intended to sit in opposite halves of the quilt. Play with them! Try different arrangements. Try rotating some blocks. Take a picture of each variation to help you decide. After you're happy with one of your arrangements, be sure to save that image. You may need it down the road to remember which block goes where.

The only other thing I knew for sure when I assembled this quilt was that I wanted the Aunt Lee's Frame blocks in the corners of the quilt. This was especially important because I had a custom label in one of these blocks. Consider where you might want your label if you incorporate it into your blocks.

1 Lay out the assembled blocks and short sashing A, B, C and D rectangles as shown in Figure 1.

2 Sew the units together into 6 rows (Figure 2).

3 Sew the rows together, making sure to sew a long sashing strip (E) between the rows. There are *no* sashing strips at the top or bottom of the quilt (only between the rows) (Figure 3).

Quilt Assembly Diagrams

Figure 1

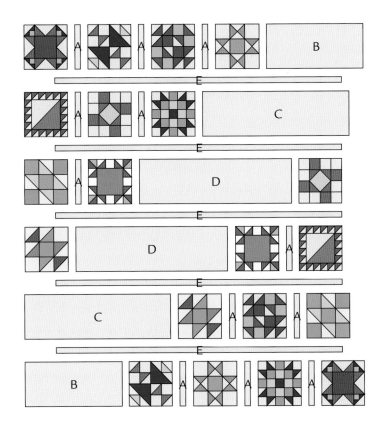

Figure 2

Figure 3

Prepare the Quilt for Finishing

THE 3 B'S: BATTING, BACKING AND BINDING

I like to have at least an extra 4" (10.2cm) of batting and backing on all four sides of a quilt. This ensures that there's enough overlap to attach the quilt to the long-arm frame if you're sending your quilt to a long-arm quilter or if you're long-arm quilting it yourself. If you're quilting on your home machine, you may not need as much overlap.

Backing

LAP QUILT (60" [152.4CM] SQUARE): Remove the selvages from the fabric and cut the total backing yardage in half lengthwise. Your 2 sections will be approximately 44" × 68" (111.8cm × 172.7cm). Cut 1 of the 2 sections to 25" × 68" (63.5cm × 172.7cm), then sew the 2 sections together along the 68" (172.7cm) side using a ½" (1.3cm) seam allowance. The backing should measure 68" (172.7cm) square (Figure 1).

TWIN QUILT (78" [198.1CM] SQUARE): Remove the selvages from the fabric and cut the total backing yardage in half lengthwise. Your 2 sections will be approximately 44"× 86" (111.8cm × 218.4cm). Sew the 2 sections together along the 86" (218.4cm) side. The backing should measure 87" × 86" (221cm × 218.4cm) (Figure 2).

SCRAPPY BACK

These instructions assume your quilt back is made with one fabric, but feel free to use several and make it scrappy. Simply use the provided measurements as a guide for the finished dimensions of your back.

Batting

Cut the batting to the same size as the backing fabric.

Binding

LAP QUILT (60" [152.4CM] SQUARE): From ½ yard (0.5m) of fabric, cut six 2½" (6.4cm) wide strips to make straight-grain double-fold continuous binding. See the Binding tutorial in Chapter 4 for details.

TWIN QUILT (78" [198.1CM]) SQUARE: From ⅝ yard (0.6m) of fabric, cut eight 2½" (6.4cm) wide strips to make straight-grain double-fold continuous binding. See the Binding tutorial in Chapter 4 for details.

Lap (Figure 1)

44" (111.8cm) 25" (63.5cm)

68" (172.7cm)

Twin (Figure 2)

44" (111.8cm) 44" (111.8cm)

86" (218.4cm)

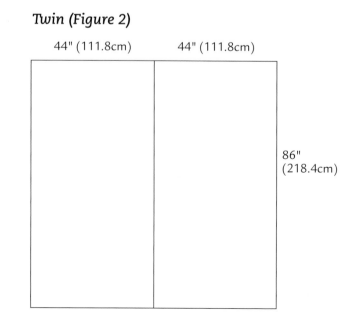

Quilting Suggestions

STRAIGHT-LINE QUILTING

Don't feel like you need an elaborate design to make your quilt look great. There are several simple straight-line quilting options for the diagonal negative space that will make your quilt look amazing.

Consider whether you want to use the same pattern in all of the quilt blocks or change the pattern for each block. You can outline the quilt with straight lines within the blocks or add more straight lines on the opposite diagonal to make a grid.

FREE-MOTION QUILTING

Depending on your confidence and skill level, there are *tons* of fun things you can do with free motion on this quilt. The sky is the limit! If you're like me, however, and you're a little shy about your free-motion skills, here are a few simple ideas.

Try the very basic cursive letter L quilting motif and stretch it across the diagonal. You can also use a clamshell motif to create simple curves.

Straight lines

Zigzag lines

The cursive L motif

The clamshell motif

Sisters' Ten Sampler Quilt

Original **SISTERS' TEN SAMPLER** by AnneMarie Chany.

SISTERS' TEN SAMPLER alternate colorway with straight-line zigzag quilting by Maureen Igusky.

Chapter 2

VICE VERSA SAMPLER

The **VICE VERSA SAMPLER** takes traditional quilt blocks, updates them with modern solid fabrics and sets them in a fun and funky diagonal setting.

The blocks used in this sampler were chosen for their polarity—the ability to construct the blocks with positive and negative space and then invert them. With each block there will be two versions: one that uses the conventional piecing of lights and darks and puts the background fabrics in the most common locations, and another that uses the background fabric as the focus of the block and puts the color in the background.

Eight of the nine blocks in the VICE VERSA SAMPLER use this concept. Working through these blocks will make you conscious of color placement within the blocks by making two versions of each block pattern.

Finished sizes:	Lap—56½" (143.5cm) square (9" [22.9cm] finished blocks) Large Twin—73½" (186.7cm) square (12" [30.5cm] finished blocks)
Number of blocks:	20 (make 2 each of 8 block patterns, 4 each of the last pattern)
Skill level:	Confident beginner—Intermediate

◄ **VICE VERSA SAMPLER**, designed, pieced and quilted by AnneMarie Chany.

These two blocks, called Rising Star, are both the Star-Within-a-Star block. They are inverse and complementary to one another, creating interesting effects when they're placed together in a quilt.

Materials

Fabric estimates are based on yardage with 42" (106.7cm) of usable fabric.
Fat quarters are 18" × 22" (45.7cm × 55.9cm).

LAP—56½" SQUARE (9" [22.9CM] FINISHED BLOCKS)

¾ yard (0.7m) each of 5 colors, or 15 fat quarters (3 fat quarters each of 5 colors)—coral, orange, lime green, putty and violet (for Fabrics B, C, D, E and F)

1¾ yards (1.6m) for block background (white solid)

2¼ yards (2.1m) for background and sashing (lavender solid)

½ yard (0.5cm) of binding fabric

3¾ yards (3.4cm) for pieced backing

66" (167.6cm) square of batting

LARGE TWIN—73½" (186.7CM) SQUARE (12" [30.5CM] FINISHED BLOCKS)

1 yard (1m) each of 5 colors, or 20 fat quarters (4 fat quarters each of 5 colors)—coral, orange, lime green, putty and violet (for Fabrics B, C, D, E and F)

2¼ yards (2.1m) of block background (white solid)

3¼ yards (3m) of background and sashing (lavender solid)

⅝ yard (0.6cm) of binding fabric

4⅝ yards (4.2m) for pieced backing

83" (210.8cm) square of batting

Fabric shown in project is Pure Elements Solids by Art Gallery Fabrics. Colors used for the sample are Snow, Coral Reef, Verve Violet, Mauvelous, Appletini, Mandarin and Macchiatto.

CUTTING INSTRUCTIONS FOR SASHING AND NEGATIVE SPACE

Cut large background pieces and sashing strips before you begin working through the blocks. Set these pieces aside until you have completed all blocks for the quilt.

FROM BACKGROUND/SASHING (LAVENDER SOLID):

For 9" (22.9cm) blocks, cut

Twenty 1½" × 9½" (3.8cm × 24.1cm) strips (SS)

One 17" (43.2cm) square (subcut on the diagonal to make 2 triangles) (A)

Three 11½" × width-of-fabric (wof) (29.2cm × wof) strips (B)

Two 1½" × wof (3.8cm × wof) strips (C)

For 12" blocks, cut

Twenty 1½" × 12½" strips (3.8cm × 31.8cm) (SS)

One 21" (53.3cm) square (subcut on the diagonal to make 2 triangles) (A)

Four 14½" × wof strips (36.8cm × wof) (B)

Three 1½" × wof strips (3.8cm × wof) (C)

Shoofly

For our first block, we're kicking it off nice and easy with the classic Shoofly block. In this block, you will make pairs of Half-Square Triangles, then use one set in Block A and the other set in Block B. Minimize the waste!

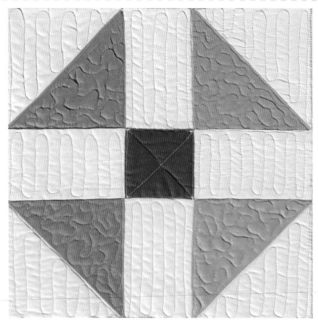

Shoofly Block A

Shoofly Block B

CUTTING INSTRUCTIONS

The cutting instructions given allow you to cut both A and B blocks at the same time. Superscript [A/B] denotes if pieces are used in block A, block B or both.

FOR 9" (22.9CM) BLOCKS

From Fabric A, cut

Four 4¾" (12.1cm) squares [A+B]

Four 2½" × 4" (6.4cm × 10.2cm) rectangles [A]

From Fabrics B, C, D and E, cut

One 4¾" (12.1cm) square [A+B]

Two 1½" × 4" (3.8cm × 10.2cm) rectangles [B]

From Fabric F, cut

Two 2½" (6.4cm) squares [A+B]

FOR 12" (30.5CM) BLOCKS

From Fabric A, cut

Four 6¼" (15.9cm) squares [A+B]

Four 2½" × 5½" (6.4cm × 14cm) rectangles [A]

From Fabrics B, C, D and E, cut

One 6¼" (15.9cm) square [A+B]

Two 1½" × 5½" (3.8cm × 14cm) rectangles [B]

From Fabric F, cut

Two 2½" (6.4cm) squares [A+B]

PIECING INSTRUCTIONS

1 Make Half-Square Triangle (HST) units, pairing 1 Fabric A square with 1 Fabric B, Fabric C, Fabric D and Fabric E square, respectively. Make 8 total HST units. See the Half-Square Triangle tutorial in Chapter 4 for details on making HSTs and squaring up. See the HSTs Yield table for quantities.

The HSTs should be trimmed to the following dimensions:
- ► 9″ (22.9cm) blocks: 4″ (10.2cm), unfinished
- ► 12″ (30.5cm) blocks: 5½″ (14cm), unfinished

HSTs Yield:
- ► 2 HSTs with Fabrics A/B
- ► 2 HSTs with Fabrics A/C
- ► 2 HSTs with Fabrics A/D
- ► 2 HSTs with Fabrics A/E

2 **BLOCK A LAYOUT.** Lay out 1 of each color of the HST units, the Fabric A rectangles and 1 Fabric F square (Figure 1).

3 Sew the units together into 3 rows (Figure 2).

4 Sew the 3 rows together to complete Block A (Figure 3). Block size: 9½″ (24.1cm) unfinished and 9″ (22.9cm) finished; 12½″ (31.8cm) unfinished and 12″ (30.5cm) finished.

5 **BLOCK B LAYOUT.** Lay out 1 of each color of the HST units, the Fabric B, C, D and E rectangles and the Fabric F square (Figure 4).

6 Repeat steps 3–4 to assemble Block B (Figure 5). Block size: 9½″ (24.1cm) unfinished and 9″ (22.9cm) finished; 12½″ (31.8cm) unfinished and 12″ (30.5cm) finished.

Figure 1

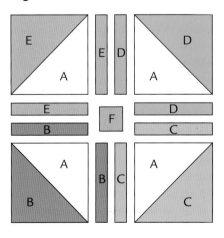

Figure 2

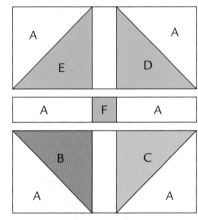

Figure 3

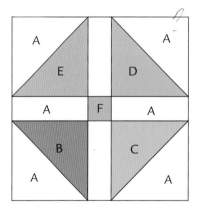

Figure 4

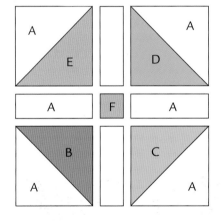

Figure 5

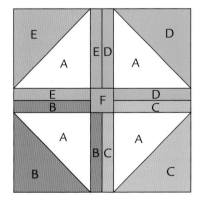

Mosaic No. 5

Half-Square Triangles are incredibly versatile. This block will help you master them while you make thirty-two total for both blocks.

Mosaic No. 5 Block A

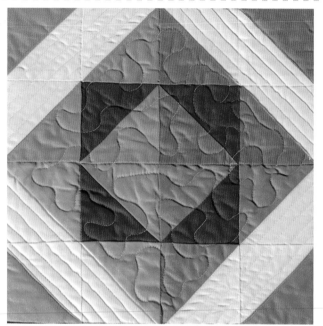

Mosaic No. 5 Block B

CUTTING INSTRUCTIONS

The cutting instructions given allow you to cut both the A and B blocks at the same time.

FOR 9" (22.9CM) BLOCKS

From Fabric A, cut
Fourteen 3½" (8.9cm) squares

From Fabrics B, C, D and E, cut
Four 3½" (8.9cm) squares

From Fabric F, cut
Six 3½" (8.9cm) squares

FOR 12" (30.5CM) BLOCKS

From Fabric A, cut
Fourteen 4¼" (10.8cm) squares

From Fabrics B, C, D and E, cut
Four 4¼" (10.8cm) squares

From Fabric F, cut
Six 4¼" (10.8cm) squares

PIECING

1 Make Half-Square Triangle (HST) units, pairing 1 Fabric A square with a Fabric B, Fabric C, Fabric D, Fabric E and Fabric F square, respectively. Make 28 total HST units. See the Half-Square Triangle tutorial in Chapter 4 for details on making HSTs and squaring up. See the HSTs Yield table for quantities.

The HSTs should be trimmed to the following dimensions:
- 9″ (22.9cm) blocks: 2¾″ (7cm), unfinished
- 12″ (30.5cm) blocks: 3½″ (8.9cm), unfinished

HSTs Yield:
- 6 HSTs with Fabrics A/B
- 6 HSTs with Fabrics A/C
- 6 HSTs with Fabrics A/D
- 6 HSTs with Fabrics A/E
- 4 HSTs with Fabrics A/F

2 Make HST units pairing 1 Fabric F square with 1 Fabric B, Fabric C, Fabric D and Fabric E square, respectively. Only 1 HST of each color will be needed for Block B (save the remainder!).

The HSTs should be squared up to the following dimensions:
- 9″ (22.9cm) blocks: 2¾″ (7cm), unfinished
- 12″ (30.5cm) blocks: 3½″ (8.9cm), unfinished

3 **BLOCK A LAYOUT.** Lay out 3 A/B HSTs, 3 A/C HSTs, 3 A/D HSTs, 3 A/E HSTs and 4 A/F HSTs (Figure 1).

4 Sew the units together into 4 rows (Figure 2).

5 Sew the 4 rows together to complete Block A (Figure 3). Block size: 9½″ (24.1cm) unfinished and 9″ (22.9cm) finished; 12½″ (31.8cm) unfinished and 12″ (30.5cm) finished.

6 **BLOCK B LAYOUT.** Lay out 3 A/B HSTs, 3 A/C HSTs, 3 A/D HSTs, 3 A/E HSTs, 1 B/F HST, 1 C/F HST, 1 D/F HST and 1 E/F HST (Figure 4).

7 Repeat steps 4–5 to assemble Block B (Figure 5). Block size: 9½″ (24.1cm) unfinished and 9″ (22.9cm) finished; 12½″ (31.8cm) unfinished and 12″ (30.5cm) finished.

Figure 1

Figure 2

Figure 3

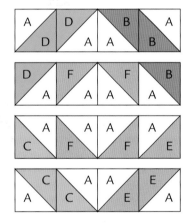

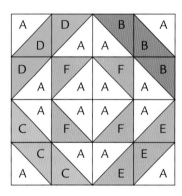

Figure 4

Figure 5

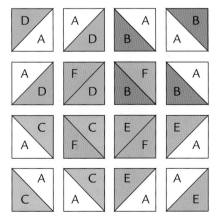

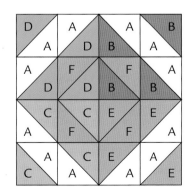

Bear's Paw

The Bear's Paw block is a beautiful classic. We're simply using Half-Square Triangles in combination with different-sized squares to make the paw shape.

Bear's Paw Block A

Bear's Paw Block B

CUTTING INSTRUCTIONS

The cutting instructions given allow you to cut both A and B blocks at the same time. Superscripts [A/B] denote whether pieces are used in block A, block B or both.

This block would also look lovely with only one color in the background of the inverse block. For the purposes of using all of our colors in quadrants for the **VICE VERSA SAMPLER**, however, I continued the theme of making the inverse block with four colored background quadrants. Don't feel as if you need to make every block this way, however. Play around and let your inspiration take you where it may!

FOR 9" (22.9CM) BLOCKS

From Fabric A, cut

Four 1¾" (4.5cm) squares [A] (small)

Sixteen 2½" (6.4cm) squares [A+B] (medium)

Four 2" × 4¼" (5.1cm × 10.8cm) rectangles [A]

Four 3" (7.6cm) squares [B] (large)

From Fabrics B, C, D and E, cut

Four 2½" (6.4cm) squares [A+B] (medium)

One 3" (7.6cm) square [A] (large)

One 1¾" (4.5cm) square [B] (small)

Two 1¼" × 4¼" (3.2cm × 10.8cm) rectangles [B]

From Fabric F, cut

Two 2" (5.1cm) squares [A+B]

FOR 12" (30.5CM) BLOCKS

From Fabric A, cut

Four 2¼" (5.7cm) squares [A] (small)

Sixteen 3" (7.6cm) squares [A+B] (medium)

Four 2" × 5¾" (5.1cm × 14.6cm) rectangles [A]

Four 4" (10.2cm) squares [B] (large)

From Fabrics B, C, D and E, cut

Four 3" (7.6cm) squares [A+B] (medium)

One 4" (10.2cm) square [A] (large)

One 2¼" (5.7cm) square [B] (small)

Four 1¼" × 5¾" (3.2cm × 14.6cm) rectangles [B]

From Fabric F, cut

Two 2" (5.1cm) squares [A+B]

PIECING

1 Make Half-Square Triangle (HST) units, pairing 1 medium Fabric A square with 1 medium Fabric B, Fabric C, Fabric D and Fabric E square, respectively. Make 32 total HST units. See the Half-Square Triangle tutorial in Chapter 4 for details on making HSTs and squaring up. See the Large HSTs Yield table for quantities.

The HSTs should be squared up to the following dimensions:
- 9" (22.9cm) blocks: 1¾" (4.5cm), unfinished
- 12" (30.5cm) blocks: 2¼" (5.7cm), unfinished

Large HSTs Yield:
- 8 HSTs with Fabrics A/B
- 8 HSTs with Fabrics A/C
- 8 HSTs with Fabrics A/D
- 8 HSTs with Fabrics A/E

2 **BLOCK A LAYOUT.** Lay out 4 A/B HSTs, 4 A/C HSTs, 4 A/D HSTs, 4 A/E HSTs, 4 small Fabric A squares, 4 Fabric A rectangles, 1 large Fabric B, C, D and E square and 1 Fabric F square (Figure 1).

3 Choose 1 color quadrant or "paw" to begin with (I began with Fabric E). Sew the 1 small Fabric A square and the 2 A/E HSTs together to form a row. Sew the remaining 2 A/E HSTs together to make a vertical row. Repeat this step for each quadrant or paw (Figure 2).

4 Starting with the Fabric E paw, sew the remaining 2 joined HSTs to the middle Fabric E square (Figure 3). Repeat with the remaining 3 paws.

Figure 1

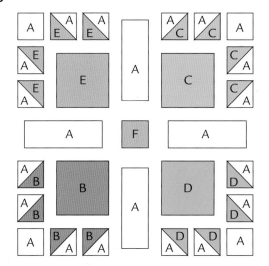

Figure 2

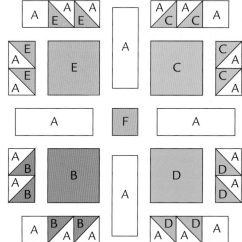

Figure 3

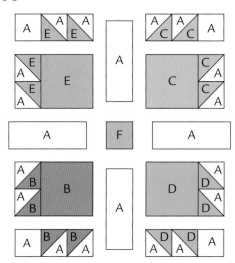

5 Starting with the Fabric E paw, sew the top row to the unit made in the previous step. Repeat with the remaining 3 paws. The paws are now complete (Figure 4).

6 The block can now be assembled into rows. Sew the units together to make 3 rows (Figure 5).

7 Sew the 3 rows together to complete Block A (Figure 6). Block size: 9½" (24.1cm) unfinished and 9" (22.9cm) finished; 12½" (31.8cm) unfinished and 12" (30.5cm) finished.

8 **BLOCK LAYOUT B.** Lay out 4 A/B HSTs, 4 A/C HSTs, 4 A/D HSTs, 4 A/E HSTs, 1 small Fabric B, C, D and E square, the narrow 2 Fabric B, C, D and E rectangles, 4 large Fabric A squares and 1 Fabric F square (Figure 7).

Figure 4

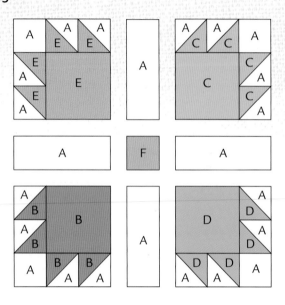

Figure 5

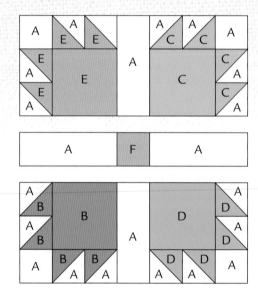

Figure 6

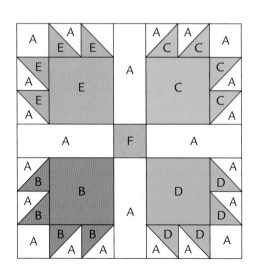

Figure 7

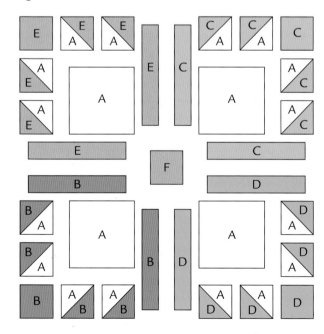

9 Assemble each paw in the same manner as Block A. Sew the 1 small Fabric E square and the 2 A/E HSTs together to form a row. Then sew the remaining 2 A/E HSTs together as shown. Sew the 2 joined HSTs to the large Fabric A square, then sew the top row to the unit. Repeat this process for each paw (Figure 8).

10 Sew the pairs of narrow rectangles together (Figure 9).

11 Sew the units together to make 3 rows (Figure 10).

12 Sew the 3 rows together to complete Block B (Figure 11). Block size: 9½" (24.1cm) unfinished and 9" (22.9cm) finished; 12½" (31.8cm) unfinished and 12" (30.5cm) finished.

Figure 8

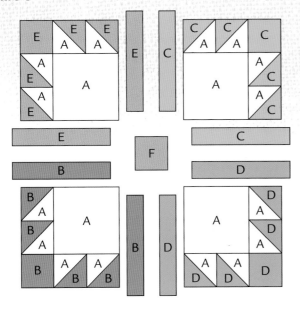

Figure 9

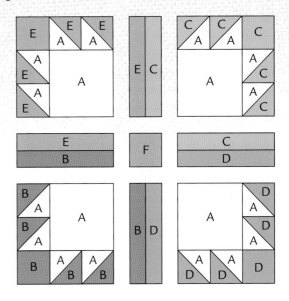

Figure 10

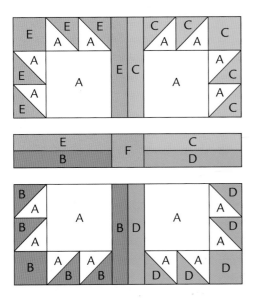

Figure 11

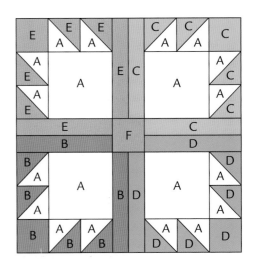

Rising Star

Almost everyone loves star blocks. Traditionally, the Rising Star uses pink fabric for the inner star, green fabric for the outer star and a white background. Simply changing how the block is colored—adding two more colors and sectioning it into quadrants— yields a new block with a completely different look.

Rising Star Block A

Rising Star Block B

CUTTING INSTRUCTIONS

The cutting instructions given allow you to cut both A and B blocks at the same time. Super-scripts A/B denote if pieces are used in block A, block B or both.

FOR 9" (22.9CM) BLOCKS

From Fabric A, cut

Eight 3½" (8.9cm) squares (large) [A+B]

Five 2¾" (7cm) squares (medium) [A]

Eight 2¼" (5.7cm) squares (small) [A+B]

Four 1⅝" (4.1cm) squares (x-small) [B]

From Fabrics B, C, D and E, cut

Two 3½" (8.9cm) squares (large) [A+B]

One 2¾" (7cm) square (medium) [B]

Two 2¼" (5.7cm) squares (small) [A+B]

Two 1⅝" (4.1cm) squares (x-small) [A+B]

FOR 12" (30.5CM) BLOCKS

From Fabric A, cut

Eight 4¼" (10.8cm) squares (large) [A+B]

Five 3½" (8.9cm) squares (medium) [A]

Eight 2¾" (7cm) squares (small) [A+B]

Four 2" (5.1cm) squares (x-small) [B]

From Fabrics B, C, D and E, cut

Two 4¼" (10.8cm) squares (large) [A+B]

One 3½" (8.9cm) square (medium) [B]

Two 2¾" (7cm) squares (small) [A+B]

Two 2" (5.1cm) squares (x-small) [A+B]

PIECING

1 Make Half-Square Triangle (HST) units pairing 1 large Fabric A square with 1 large Fabric B, Fabric C, Fabric D and Fabric E square, respectively. Make 16 total HST units. See the Half-Square Triangle tutorial in Chapter 4 for details on making HSTs and squaring up. See the Large HSTs Yield table for quantities.

The HSTs should be squared to the following dimensions:
- ▶ 9″ (22.9cm) blocks: 2¾″ (7cm), unfinished
- ▶ 12″ (30.5cm) blocks: 3½″ (8.9cm) unfinished

Large HSTs Yield:
- ▶ 4 HSTs with Fabrics A/B
- ▶ 4 HSTs with Fabrics A/C
- ▶ 4 HSTs with Fabrics A/D
- ▶ 4 HSTs with Fabrics A/E

2 Make HST units pairing 1 small Fabric A square with 1 small Fabric B, Fabric C, Fabric D and Fabric E square, respectively. Make 16 total HST units. See the Small HSTs Yield table for quantities.

The HSTs should be squared up to the following dimensions:
- ▶ 9″ (22.9cm) blocks: 1⅝″ (4.1cm), unfinished
- ▶ 12″ (30.5cm) blocks: 2″ (5.1cm), unfinished

Small HSTs Yield:
- ▶ 4 HSTs with Fabrics A/B
- ▶ 4 HSTs with Fabrics A/C
- ▶ 4 HSTs with Fabrics A/D
- ▶ 4 HSTs with Fabrics A/E

3 BLOCK A LAYOUT. Lay out 5 medium Fabric A squares, 2 large and 2 small A/B HSTs, 2 large and 2 small A/C HSTs, 2 large and 2 small A/D HSTs, 2 large and 2 small A/E HSTs, and the x-small Fabric B, C, D and E squares (Figure 1).

4 Piece the inside star first. Sew the top row together (Fabric D square, A/D HST, A/B HST and Fabric B square). Repeat the process for the bottom row. Sew the A/C and A/D HSTs together on the left side. Repeat for the right side. Sew the pairs of HSTs to the respective left and right sides of the center block, then sew the top and bottom rows to complete the inside star.

*Inside star is 5″ (12.7cm) square, unfinished for 9″ (22.9cm) blocks; 6½″ (16.5cm) square, unfinished for 12″ (30.5cm) blocks.

5 Piece the outside star. Sew the 4 units in the top row together. Repeat for the bottom row. Sew the 2 HST units on the left side together and repeat for the right side (Figure 2).

Figure 1

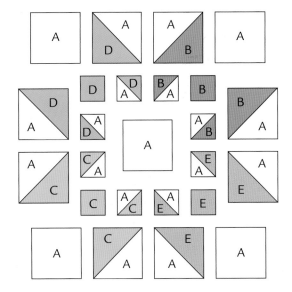

Figure 2

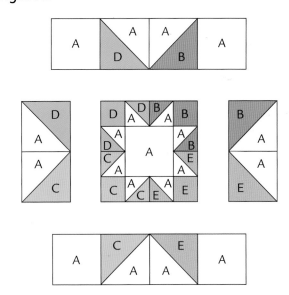

6 Sew the 2 HST pair units to the left and right sides of the inner star. Sew the top and bottom rows to the unit to complete Block A (Figure 3). Press all seams.

Block size: 9½" (24.1cm) unfinished and 9" (22.9cm) finished; 12½" (31.8cm) unfinished and 12" (30.5cm) finished.

7 **BLOCK B LAYOUT.** Lay out 2 large and 2 small A/B HSTs, 2 large and 2 small A/C HSTs, 2 large and 2 small A/D HSTs, 2 large and 2 small A/E HSTs, 1 x-small Fabric B, C, D and E square, 4 x-small Fabric A squares and 1 medium Fabric B, C, D and E square (Figure 4).

8 Again, assemble the inner star first. Sew the 1⅝" (4.1cm) squares and HSTs into 4 rows (Figure 5). Press.

Figure 3

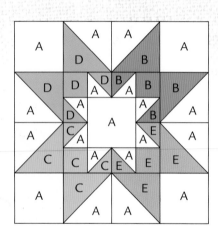

Figure 4

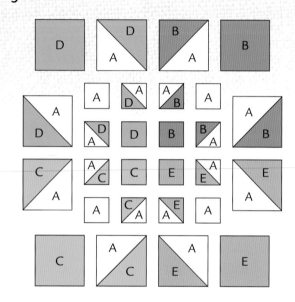

Figure 5

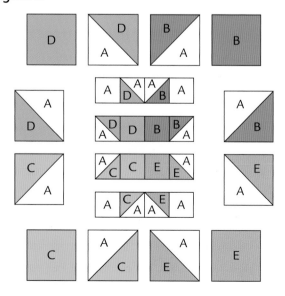

9 Next, sew the 4 rows together to form the inner star (Figure 6).

*Inside star is 5″ (12.7cm) square unfinished for 9″ (22.9cm) blocks; 6½″ (16.5cm) square unfinished for 12″ (30.5cm) blocks.

10 Piece the outside star. Sew the 4 units in the top row together. Repeat for the bottom row. Sew the 2 HST units on the left side together and repeat for the right side (Figure 7).

11 Sew the left and right pairs of HSTs to the respective left and right sides of the inside star block. Complete Block B by sewing the top and bottom rows to the previous unit (Figure 8). Press all seams.

Block size: 9½″ (24.1cm) unfinished and 9″ (22.9cm) finished; 12½″ (31.8cm) unfinished and 12″ (30.5cm) finished.

Figure 6

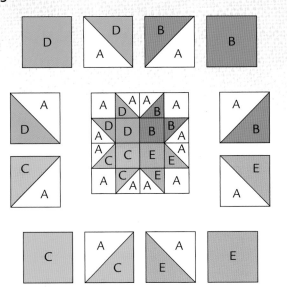

Figure 7

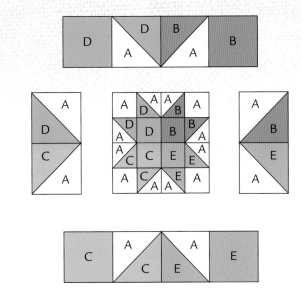

Figure 8

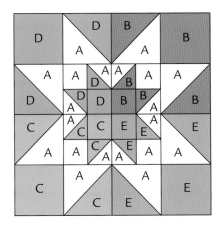

Mosaic No. 2

This block is a slight variation of Mosaic No. 5. This time you will use Flying Geese units to construct the block instead of solely relying on Half-Square Triangles. Hooray for Geese! Flying Geese is another great quilting fundamental to add to your repertoire.

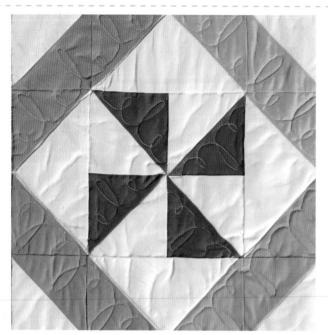

Mosaic No. 2 Block A

Mosaic No. 2 Block B

CUTTING INSTRUCTIONS

The cutting instructions given allow you to cut both A and B blocks at the same time. Superscripts ᴬ/ᴮ denote if pieces are used in block A, block B or both.

As you cut each fabric, label the cuts with the place they will be used: HST or FG for Flying Geese. It will help to keep pieces organized if you have two plastic baggies: one for HSTs and one for FG.

FOR 9" (22.9CM) BLOCKS

From Fabric A, cut

Ten 3½" (8.9cm) squares (large, HSTs) ᴬ⁺ᴮ

Four 2¾" × 5" (7cm × 12.7cm) rectangles (FG) ᴬ

Eight 2¾" (7cm) squares (small, FG) ᴮ

From Fabrics B, C, D and E, cut

Two 3½" (8.9cm) squares (large, HSTs) ᴬ⁺ᴮ

Two 2¾" (7cm) squares (small, FG) ᴬ

From Fabric F, cut

Four 2¾" × 5" (7cm × 12.7cm) rectangles (FG) ᴮ

Two 3½" (8.9cm) squares (large, HSTs) ᴬ

FOR 12" (30.5CM) BLOCKS

From Fabric A, cut

Ten 4¼" (10.8cm) squares (large, HSTs) ᴬ⁺ᴮ

Four 3½" × 6½" (8.9cm × 16.5cm) rectangles (FG) ᴬ

Eight 3½" (8.9cm) squares (small, FG) ᴮ

From Fabrics B, C, D and E, cut

Two 4¼" (10.8cm) squares (large, HSTs) ᴬ⁺ᴮ

Two 3½" (8.9cm) squares (small, FG) ᴬ

From Fabric F, cut

Four 3½" × 6½" (8.9cm × 16.5cm) rectangles (FG) ᴮ

Two 4¼" (10.8cm) squares (large, HSTs) ᴮ

PIECING

1 Make Half-Square Triangle (HST) units, pairing 1 large Fabric A square with 1 large Fabric B, Fabric C, Fabric D, Fabric E and Fabric F square, respectively. Make 20 total HST units. See the Half-Square Triangle tutorial in Chapter 4 for details on making HSTs and squaring up. See the HSTs Yield table for quantities.

The HSTs should be squared to the following dimensions:
- ► 9″ (22.9cm) blocks: 2¾″ (7cm), unfinished
- ► 12″ (30.5cm) blocks: 3½″ (8.9cm), unfinished

HSTs Yield:
- ► 4 HSTs with Fabrics A/B
- ► 4 HSTs with Fabrics A/C
- ► 4 HSTs with Fabrics A/D
- ► 4 HSTs with Fabrics A/E
- ► 4 HSTs with Fabrics A/F

2 Make Flying Geese units for Block B. Use 8 small Fabric A squares with 4 Fabric F rectangles. Make 4 total Flying Geese units. See the Flying Geese tutorial in Chapter 4 for details on making Flying Geese.

The Flying Geese should measure the following dimensions:
- ► 9″ (22.9cm) blocks: 2¾″ × 5″ (7cm × 12.7cm), unfinished
- ► 12″ (30.5cm) blocks: 3½″ × 6½″ (8.9cm × 16.5cm), unfinished

3 Make Flying Geese units for Block A. Use 2 small squares of each fabric B, C, D and E and 4 Fabric A rectangles. Make 4 total Flying Geese units: 1 each of the 4 color combinations shown (Figure 1). Pay special attention to whether each color is placed on the left or right side.

The Flying Geese should measure the following dimensions:
9″ (22.9cm) blocks: 2¾″ × 5″ (7cm × 12.7cm), unfinished
12″ (30.5cm) blocks: 3½″ × 6½″ (8.9cm × 16.5cm), unfinished

Figure 1

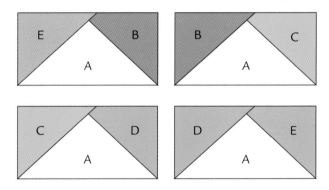

Make 1 unit of each variant

LEFTOVER HALF-SQUARE TRIANGLES

Note that this method of making Half-Square Triangles will result in extra units for the A/B, A/C, A/D and A/E color combinations. The extra units will not be used in this project and can be saved or discarded, as you prefer.

4 **BLOCK A LAYOUT.** Lay out 4 A/F HSTs, 1 A/B HST, 1 A/C HST, 1 A/D HST, 1 A/E HST and the 4 colorful Flying Geese units from step 3 (Figure 2).

5 First, sew the A/F HSTs into 2 rows, then sew those rows together to make a pinwheel. Also, sew 1 of the A/B and A/C HSTs and 1 A/B/C Flying Geese unit together to make the top row. Then sew 1 of the A/D and A/E HSTs and 1 A/D/E Flying Geese unit together to make the bottom row (Figure 3).

6 Sew the remaining 2 Flying Geese units to the left and right sides of the center pinwheel (Figure 4).

7 Sew the top and bottom rows to the unit to complete Block A (Figure 5).
Block size: 9½" (24.1cm) unfinished and 9" (22.9cm) finished; 12½" (31.8cm) unfinished and 12" (30.5cm) finished.

Figure 2

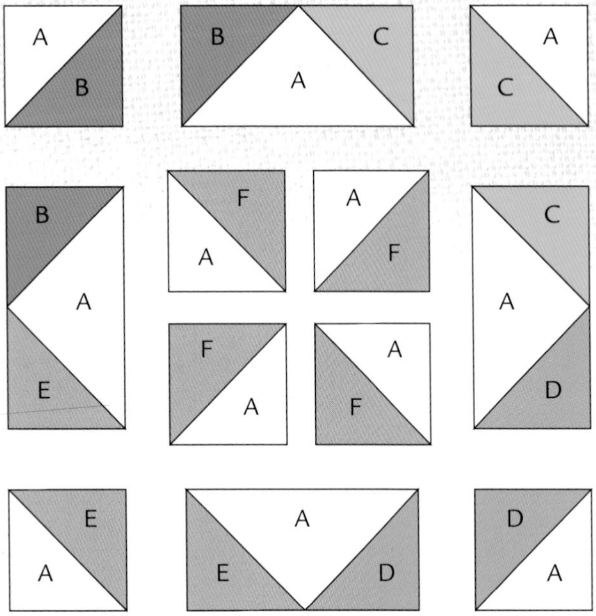

Figure 3

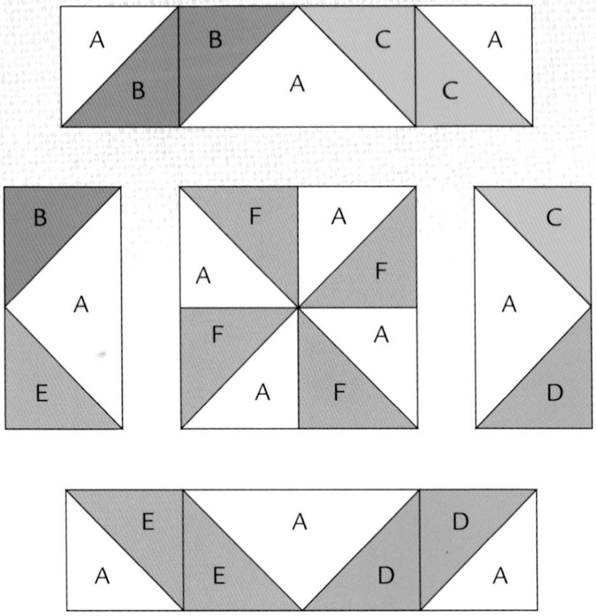

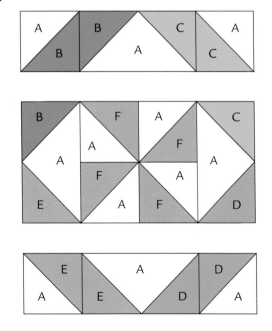

Figure 4

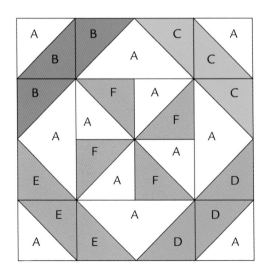

Figure 5

8 **BLOCK B LAYOUT.** Lay out 4 A/F Flying Geese, 2 A/B HSTs, 2 A/C HSTs, 2 A/D HSTs and 2 A/E HSTs (Figure 6).

9 Repeat steps 5–7 to complete Block B (Figure 7).
Block size: 9½″ (24.1cm) unfinished and 9″ (22.9cm) finished; 12½″(31.8cm) unfinished and 12″ (30.5cm) finished.

Figure 6

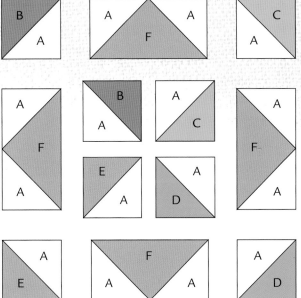

Figure 7

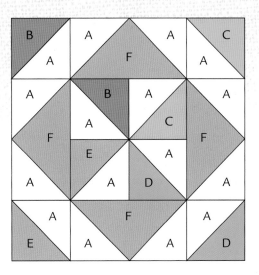

" BLOCKS
mostly done 2-20-17
osaic #5 cut 28" HST sew
RIM 2-21-17
Pillot cut 2-21-17 10PM
Sew 2-28-17 r
m-sew Mosaic 3-9-17 1-3PM
7 3-5 PM cut Bear Paw
5-5:30 pc 4 blocks
17 finished both 2:30PM
cut Rising Star finish 1 3-13-17
BACKGROUND WH
CORAL
PINK ORANGE
LIME
YELLOW
TURQUOISE

57

Capital T

This block is a great example of a block that could be sewn with all Half-Square Triangles. We use Flying Geese where we can to minimize the number of units in each block. You will make this block with Flying Geese in Block A, but you will use HSTs in Block B. Make sure to pay attention to where the colors are placed to maintain the correct pattern.

Capital T Block A

Capital T Block B

CUTTING INSTRUCTIONS

The cutting instructions given allow you to cut both A and B blocks at the same time. Superscripts [A/B] denote if pieces are used in block A, block B or both.

As you cut each fabric, label the cuts with the place they will be used: HST or FG for Flying Geese. It will help to keep pieces organized if you have two plastic baggies: one for HSTs and one for FG.

FOR 9" (22.9CM) BLOCKS:

From Fabric A, cut

Four 4¼" (10.8cm) squares (large HSTs) [A+B]

One 3½" (8.9cm) square (center) [A]

Eight 2 ×"3½" (5.1cm × 8.9cm) rectangles (FG) [A]

Eight 2¾" (7cm) squares (small HSTs) [B]

From Fabrics B, C, D and E, cut

One 4¼" (10.8cm) square (large HSTs) [A+B]

Two 2¾" (7cm) squares (small HSTs) [B]

Five 2" (5.1cm) squares (4 FG[A]; 1 center[B]) [A+B]

FOR 12" (30.5CM) BLOCKS:

From Fabric A, cut

Four 5¼" (13.3cm) squares (large HST) [A+B]

One 4½" (11.4cm) square (center) [A]

Eight 2½" × 4½" (11.4cm × 6.4cm) rectangles (FG) [A]

Eight 3¼" (8.3cm) squares (small HSTs) [B]

From Fabrics B, C, D and E, cut

One 5¼" (13.3cm) square (large HSTs) [A+B]

Two 3¼" (8.3cm) squares (small HSTs) [B]

Five 2½" (6.4cm) squares (4 FG[A]; 1 center[B]) [A+B]

PIECING

1 Make Half-Square Triangle (HST) units, pairing 1 large Fabric A square with 1 large Fabric B, Fabric C, Fabric D and Fabric E square, respectively. Make 8 total HST units. See the Half-Square Triangle tutorial in Chapter 4 for details on making HSTs and squaring up. See the Large HSTs Yield table for quantities.

The HSTs should be squared to the following dimensions:
- 9″ (22.9cm) blocks: 3½″ (8.9cm), unfinished
- 12″ (30.5cm) blocks: 4½″ (11.4cm), unfinished

Large HSTs Yield:
- 2 HSTs with Fabrics A/B
- 2 HSTs with Fabrics A/C
- 2 HSTs with Fabrics A/D
- 2 HSTs with Fabrics A/E

2 Make HST units, pairing 1 small Fabric A square with 1 large Fabric B, Fabric C, Fabric D and Fabric E square, respectively. Make 16 total HST units. See the Small HSTs Yield table for quantities.

The HSTs should be squared to the following dimensions:
- 9″ (22.9cm) blocks: 2″ (5.1cm), unfinished
- 12″ (30.5cm) blocks: 2½″ (6.4cm), unfinished

Small HSTs Yield:
- 4 HSTs with Fabrics A/B
- 4 HSTs with Fabrics A/C
- 4 HSTs with Fabrics A/D
- 4 HSTs with Fabrics A/E

3 Make Flying Geese units for Block A. Use 4 squares cut for Flying Geese of each Fabric B, C, D and E, and 8 Fabric A rectangles. Make 8 total Flying Geese units: 2 each of the 4 color combinations shown in Figure 1. See the Flying Geese tutorial in Chapter 4 for details on making Flying Geese. Pay special attention to whether each color is placed on the left or right side.

The Flying Geese should measure the following dimensions:
- 9″ (22.9cm) blocks: 2″ × 3½″ (5.1cm × 8.9cm), unfinished
- 12″ (30.5cm) blocks: 2½″ × 4½″ (6.4cm × 11.4cm), unfinished

Figure 1

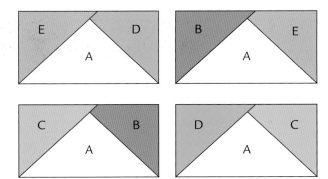

Make 2 units of each variant

4 **BLOCK A LAYOUT.** Lay out 1 Fabric A center, 1 large A/B HST, 1 large A/C HST, 1 large A/D HST, 1 large A/E HST and the 8 colorful Flying Geese units from step 3 (Figure 2).

5 First, sew the Flying Geese units into pairs (Figure 3).

6 Sew the units together to make 3 rows (Figure 4).

7 Sew the rows together to complete Block A (Figure 5). Block size: 9½" (24.1cm) unfinished and 9" (22.9cm) finished; 12½" (31.8cm) unfinished and 12" (30.5cm) finished.

Figure 2

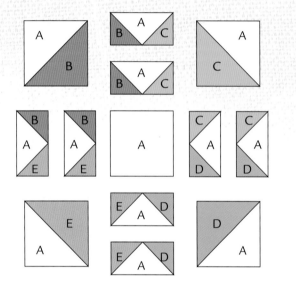

Figure 3

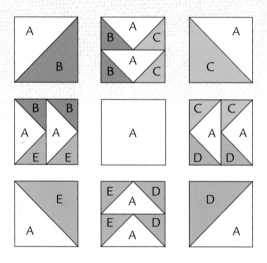

Figure 4

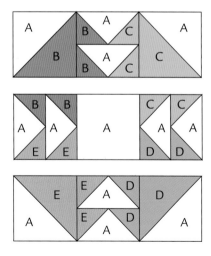

Figure 5

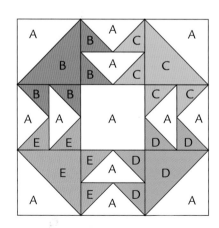

60

8 **BLOCK B LAYOUT.** Lay out the small HST units, 4 remaining large HST units, and the remaining Fabric B, C, D and E squares. Begin by sewing the small HST units together into pairs (Figure 6).

9 Sew the 4 center squares into a Four-Patch block, then sew the HST pairs together into Four-Patch blocks (Figure 7).

10 Sew the units together into 3 rows (Figure 8).

11 Sew the 3 rows together to complete Block B (Figure 9). Block size: 9½" (24.1cm) unfinished and 9" (22.9cm) finished; 12½" (31.8cm) unfinished and 12" (30.5cm) finished.

Figure 6

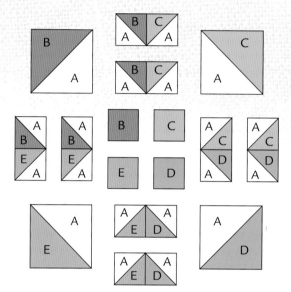

Figure 7

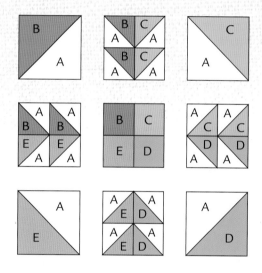

Figure 8

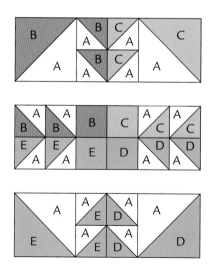

Figure 9

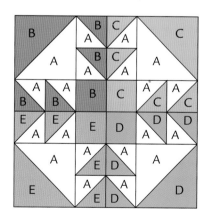

61

Fox & Geese

The Fox & Geese block certainly looks like a goose chase. Don't be intimidated by all those geese! We'll make the Flying Geese units by trying a time- and waste-saving technique that will make four geese at once. It's a fun method to use when you need several geese of the same color.

Fox & Geese Block A

Fox & Geese Block B

CUTTING INSTRUCTIONS

The cutting instructions given allow you to cut both A and B blocks at the same time. Superscripts A/B denote if pieces are used in block A, block B or both.

As you cut each fabric, label the cuts with the place they will be used: HST and FG for Flying Geese. This will help keep the pieces organized. I also recommend using plastic baggies to keep the pieces separate.

FOR 9" (22.9CM) BLOCKS

From Fabric A, cut
Ten 3½" (8.9cm) squares (large)
**Use 4 for Geese B

**Use 6 for HSTs A+B
One 5" (12.7cm) square (center) A
Sixteen 2" (5.1cm) squares (small FG) A

From Fabrics B, C, D and E, cut
Two 3½" (8.9cm) squares (large)
**Use 1 for Geese in Block A
**Use 1 for HST in Block B
Four 2" (5.1cm) squares (small FG) B

From Fabric F, cut
One 5" (12.7cm) square (center) B
Two 3½" (8.9cm) squares (large HSTs) A

FOR 12" (30.5CM) BLOCKS

From Fabric A, cut
Ten 4¼" (10.8cm) squares (large)

**Use 4 for Geese B
**Use 6 for HSTs A+B
One 6½" (16.5cm) square (center) A
Sixteen 2⅜" (6cm) squares (small FG) A

From Fabrics B, C, D and E, cut
Two 4¼" (10.8cm) squares
**Use 1 for Geese in block A
**Use 1 for HSTs in block B
Four 2⅜" (6cm) squares (small FG) B

From Fabric F, cut
One 6½" (16.5cm) square (center) B
Two 4¼" (10.8cm) squares (small HSTs) A

PIECING

1 Make Half-Square Triangle (HST) units, pairing the large HST squares for Fabric A with the large Fabric B, Fabric C, Fabric D, Fabric E and Fabric F squares, respectively. Make 12 total HST units. See the Half-Square Triangle tutorial in Chapter 4 for details on making HSTs and squaring up. See the HSTs Yield Table for quantities.

The HSTs should be squared to the following dimensions:
- ▶ 9" (22.9cm) blocks: 2¾" (7cm), unfinished
- ▶ 12" (30.9cm) blocks: 3½" (8.9cm), unfinished

HSTs Yield:
- ▶ 2 HSTs with Fabrics A/B*
- ▶ 2 HSTs with Fabrics A/C*
- ▶ 2 HSTs with Fabrics A/D*
- ▶ 2 HSTs with Fabrics A/E*
- ▶ 4 HSTs with Fabrics A/F

*We will only need 1 HST unit of the 2 for Block B. Set aside the extra HST.

2 Make No-Waste Flying Geese units for Block A using 1 large Fabric B, C, D or E square and 4 small Fabric A squares. Make 16 total Flying Geese units: 4 each of the 4 color combinations shown in Figure 1. See the No-Waste Flying Geese tutorial in Chapter 4 for details on making 4 Flying Geese at a time.

The Flying Geese should measure the following dimensions:
- ▶ 9" (22.9cm) blocks: 1⅝" × 2¾" (4.1cm × 7cm) unfinished
- ▶ 12" (30.5cm) blocks: 2" × 3½" (5.1cm × 8.9cm) unfinished

3 Make No-Waste Flying Geese units for Block B. One large Fabric A square and 4 small Fabric B, C, D or E squares will make 4 No-Waste Flying Geese. Make 16 total Flying Geese units: 4 each of the 4 color combinations shown in Figure 2.

The Flying Geese should measure the following dimensions:
- ▶ 9" (22.9cm) blocks: 1⅝" × 2¾" (4.1cm × 7cm), unfinished
- ▶ 12" (30.5cm) blocks: 2" × 3½" (5.1cm × 8.9cm), unfinished

Figure 1

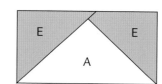
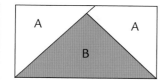
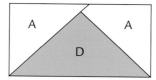
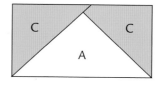

Make 4 units of each variant

Figure 2

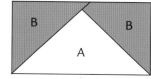
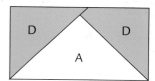

Make 4 units of each variant

4 **BLOCK A LAYOUT.** Lay out 4 A/F HSTs, 4 A/B Flying Geese, 4 A/C Flying Geese, 4 A/D Flying Geese, 4 A/E Flying Geese and the Fabric A center (Figure 3).

5 First, sew the Flying Geese units of the same color together (Figure 4).

6 Sew the units together to make 3 rows (Figure 5).

7 Sew the 3 rows together to complete Block A (Figure 6). Block size: 9½" (24.1cm) unfinished and 9" (22.9cm) finished; 12½" (31.8cm) unfinished and 12" (30.5cm) finished.

Figure 3

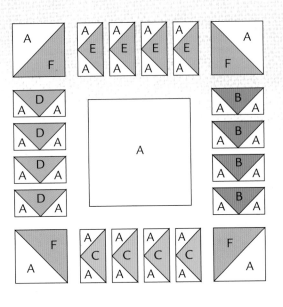

Figure 4

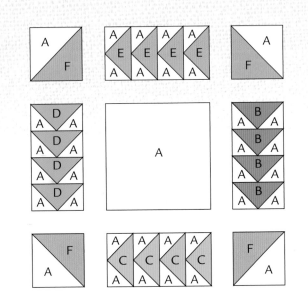

Figure 5

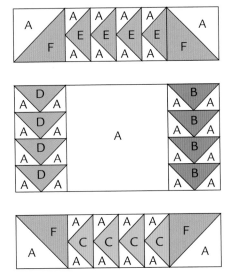

Figure 6

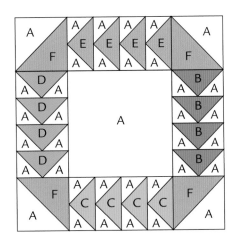

8 **BLOCK B LAYOUT.** Lay out 1 A/B, A/C, A/D and A/E HST, 4 A/B Flying Geese, 4 A/C Flying Geese, 4 A/D Flying Geese, 4 A/E Flying Geese and the Fabric F center (Figure 7).

9 Repeat steps 5–7 to assemble Block B (Figure 8). Block size: 9½" (24.1cm) unfinished and 9" (22.9cm) finished; 12½" (31.8cm) unfinished and 12" (30.5cm) finished.

Figure 7

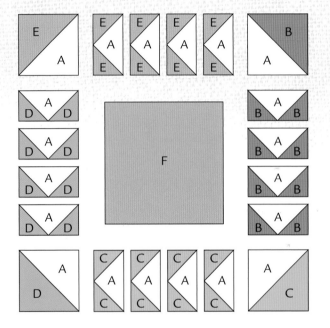

Figure 8

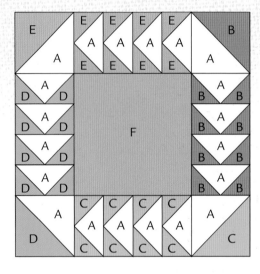

Arkansas Snowflake

This is a beautiful block, but sometimes beauty doesn't come easily! For this block, we'll be making one Hourglass block, a few Stitch-n-Flip blocks and using pieced templates. Don't worry—each individual portion of the block is relatively simple with few pieces.

Arkansas Snowflake Block A

Arkansas Snowflake Block B

CUTTING INSTRUCTIONS

The cutting instructions given allow you to cut both A and B blocks at the same time. Superscripts ^A/B denote whether pieces are used in Block A, Block B or both.

FOR 9" (22.9CM) BLOCKS

From Fabric A, cut

Five 3½" (8.9cm) squares (center)

**Use 1 for center in Block ^A

**Use 4 for Block ^B (large)

4 Template C ^B

Arkansas Snowflake templates are located on pages 70–71.

4 Template D ^B
4 Template E ^A
Four 2⅜" (6cm) squares (small) ^A

From Fabrics B, C, D and F, cut
One 3½" (8.9cm) square (large) ^A

1 Template C ^A
1 Template D ^A
1 Template E ^B
One 2⅜" (6cm) square (small) ^B
One 4¼" (10.8cm) square (Hourglass)* ^B

*Subcut on both diagonals to make 4 triangles. (We will use only 1 of the triangles in each color.)

FOR 12" (30.5CM) BLOCKS

From Fabric A, cut

Five 4½" (11.4cm) squares

**Use 1 for center in block ^A

**Use 4 for block ^B (large).

4 Template C ^B
4 Template D ^B
4 Template E ^A
Four 2⅞" (7.3cm) squares (small) ^A

From Fabrics B, C, D and F, cut
One 4½" (11.4cm) square (large) ^A

1 Template C ^A
1 Template D ^A
1 Template E ^B

One 2⅞" (7.3cm) square (small) ^B

One 5¼" (13.3cm) square (Hourglass)* ^B

*Subcut on both diagonals to make 4 triangles. (We will use only 1 of the triangles in each color.)

66

PIECING

1 Make Stitch-n-Flip units for Blocks A and B. Pair 1 large Fabric B square with 1 small Fabric A square to make 1 Stitch-n-Flip unit. Draw a diagonal line on the wrong side of the small Fabric A square. Layer the Fabric A square atop the top left corner of the Fabric B square with right sides together. Sew on the drawn line, then trim the excess by cutting ¼" (6mm) away from the stitching. Press the corner open to complete the unit (Figure 1).

Stitch-n-Flip units should measure the following dimensions:

▸ 9" (22.9cm) blocks: 3½" (8.9cm), unfinished
▸ 12" (30.5cm) blocks: 4½" (11.4cm), unfinished

2 Make all 8 Stitch-n-Flip units. Repeat the same procedure used in step 1 to make Stitch-n-Flip units using the fabric combinations shown in Figure 2.

3 **ASSEMBLE TEMPLATE UNITS.** Use 1 Fabric B Template E, 1 Fabric A Template C and 1 Fabric A Template D to make 1 template unit (Figure 3).

Flip Template D over along the triangle's diagonal and place right sides together on top of Template E. The clipped corners at the top and bottom corners of the unit help you position and align the templates. Make sure the clipped corners match as shown on the left side. Pin the pieces in place and sew. Press the unit open as shown on the right side (Figures 4 and 5).

Figure 1

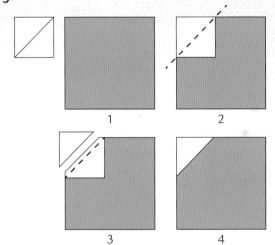

Figure 2

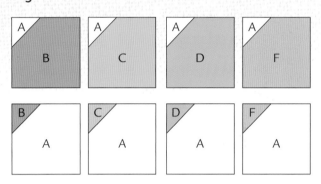

Make 1 unit of each variant.

Figure 3

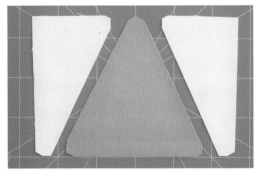

Figure 4

align notches

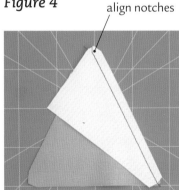

Figure 5

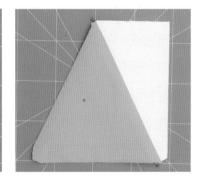

Repeat the same procedure for Template C to finish the block (Figures 6 and 7).

Template units should measure the following dimensions:
- ▶ 9″ (22.9cm) block: 3½″ (8.9cm), unfinished
- ▶ 12″ (30.5cm) blocks: 4½″ (11.4cm), unfinished

4 Make 8 template units. Repeat step 3 to make template units using the fabric combinations in Figure 8. Make 1 unit of each variant.

5 Make an Hourglass block for the center of Block B. Lay out 1 Hourglass triangle of Fabrics B, C, D and F. First, sew the Fabric B and Fabric F triangles together, then sew the Fabric C and Fabric D triangles together. Sew the Fabric B/F triangle to the Fabric C/D triangle to complete the Hourglass block (Figure 9). Be sure to pin when sewing triangles. See the Quarter Square Triangle tutorial in Chapter 4 for details on squaring up.

Square the Hourglass block to the following dimensions:
- ▶ 9″ (22.9cm) block: 3½″ (8.9cm) square, unfinished
- ▶ 12″ (30.5cm) block: 4½″ (11.4cm) square, unfinished

Figure 6

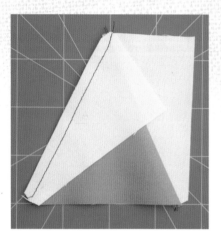

Figure 7

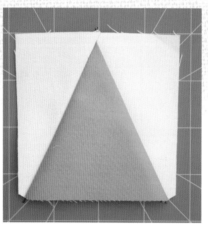

Figure 8

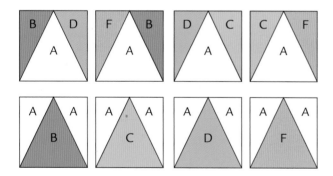

Make 1 unit of each variant

Figure 9

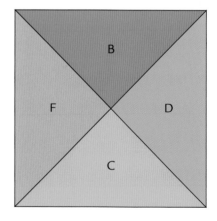

6 **BLOCK A LAYOUT.** Lay out 4 Stitch-n-Flip blocks, 4 Color Combination Template blocks and 1 Fabric A center (Figure 10).

7 Sew the units together to make 3 rows.

8 Sew the 3 rows together to complete Block A (Figure 11). Block size: 9½" (24.1cm) unfinished and 9" (22.9cm) finished; 12½" (31.8cm) unfinished and 12" (30.5cm) finished.

9 **BLOCK B LAYOUT.** Lay out 4 Stitch-n-Flip blocks, 4 Color Combination Template blocks and 1 Hourglass Center (Figure 12).

10 Repeat steps 7–8 to assemble Block B (Figures 13 and 14). Block size: 9½" (24.1cm) unfinished and 9" (22.9cm) finished; 12½" (31.8cm) unfinished and 12" (30.5cm) finished.

Figure 10

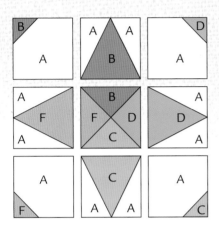

Figure 11

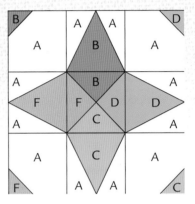

Figure 12

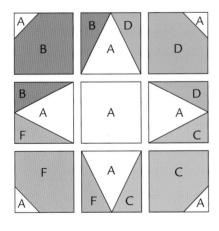

Figure 13

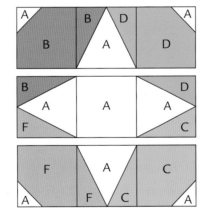

Figure 14

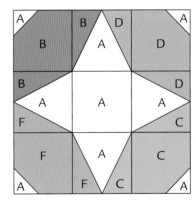

Templates

9" (22.9CM) ARKANSAS SNOWFLAKE TEMPLATES

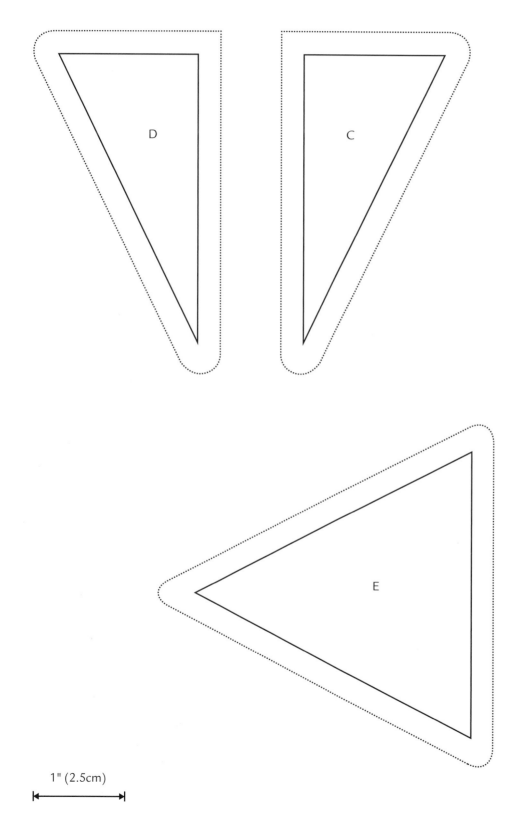

1" (2.5cm)

12" (30.5CM) ARKANSAS SNOWFLAKE TEMPLATES

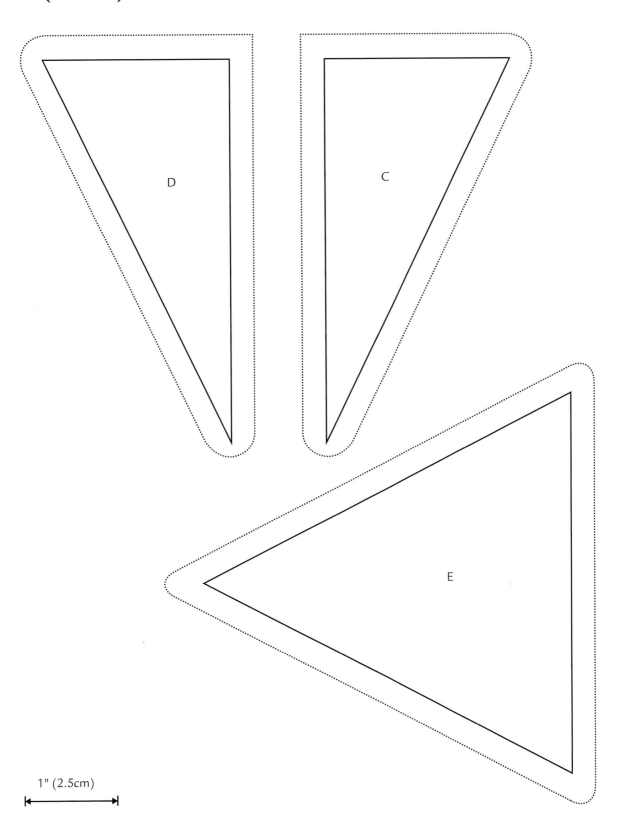

D

C

E

1" (2.5cm)

Striped Corner

This striped setting block bookends the intricate blocks we've made for this sampler quilt. It's easy to make using strip piecing. Make four striped blocks and cut each of those on the diagonal to make eight setting triangles. It's a simple yet stunning way to showcase your work!

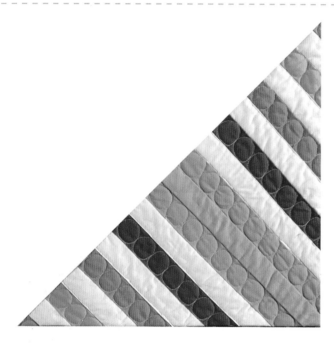

**Striped Corner
Block A**

CUTTING INSTRUCTIONS

FOR 9" (22.9CM) BLOCKS

From Fabric A, cut
Four 1½" × wof (3.8cm × wof) strips

From Fabrics B, C, D and F, cut
One 1½" × wof (3.8cm × wof) strip

From Fabric D, cut
One 1⅞" × wof (4.8cm × wof) strip

FOR 12" (30.5CM) BLOCKS

From Fabric A, cut
Eight 1¾" × wof (4.5cm × wof) strips

From Fabrics B, C, D and F, cut
Two 1¾" × wof (4.5cm × wof) strips

From Fabric D, cut
Two 2½" × wof (6.4cm × wof) strips

PIECING

1 Make a strip set. Sew the width-of-fabric (wof) strips together along the long side. For 9″ (22.9cm) blocks, make 1 strip set. For 12″ (30.5cm) blocks, make 2 strip sets. Reference Figure 1 for color placement.

2 Cut the strip set(s) into 4 segments. Each segment should be a square (Figure 1).

Strip segment squares should measure the following dimensions:

- ▸ 9″ (22.9cm) blocks: 9⅞″ (25.1cm) square, unfinished
- ▸ 12″ (30.5cm) blocks: 12⅞″ (32.7cm) square, unfinished

3 Cut each of the 4 blocks on the diagonal to make triangles. Be careful which way you cut the diagonal! To have the stripes all running in the same direction, you will need to cut 2 of the 4 blocks from the top left corner to the bottom right corner and 2 of the blocks from the top right corner to the bottom left corner (Figure 2).

Figure 1

9⅞″ (25.1cm) or 12⅞″ (32.7cm)

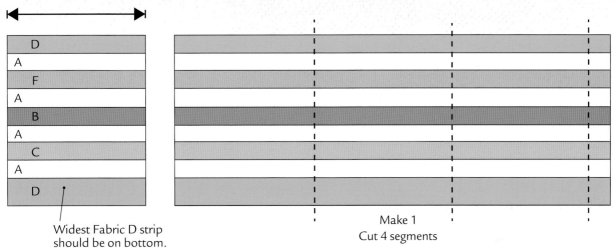

Widest Fabric D strip should be on bottom.

Make 1
Cut 4 segments

Figure 2

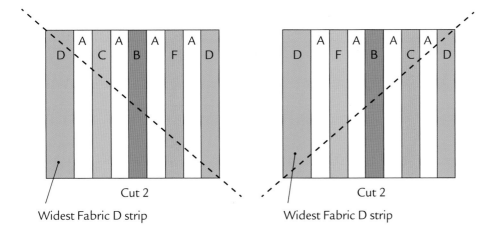

Cut 2

Widest Fabric D strip

Cut 2

Widest Fabric D strip

Assemble the Sashing

Using the large background pieces and sashing you set aside from the Cutting Instructions for Sashing and Negative Space, make and label the pieces as follows (also, see the Quilt Assembly Diagram):

FOR 9" (22.9CM) BLOCKS

SS: short sashing strip (1½" × 9½" [3.8cm × 24.1cm])

Section A: 17" (43.2cm) subcut triangle

Section B: 11½" × 64" (29.2cm × 162.6cm)

TO MAKE B SECTIONS

Remove selvages from all three 11½" × wof (29.2cm × wof) strips. Cut one 11½" × wof (29.2cm × wof) strip in half lengthwise. Sew one 11½" × 20" (29.2cm × 50.8cm) and one 11½" × wof (29.2cm × wof) strip together to make one 11½" × 64" (29.2cm × 62.6cm) strip. Repeat to yield two 11½" × 64" (29.2cm × 162.6cm) strips. 64" (162.6cm) is a minimum, so don't worry if your strips are longer. We need excess on both ends of the strip for squaring up.

Section C: 1½" × 88" (3.8cm × 223.5cm)

TO MAKE C SECTIONS

Remove selvages from both 1½" × wof (3.8cm × wof) strips. Sew the strips together to make one 1½" × 88" (3.8cm × 223.5cm) strip. Again, we need excess on both ends of the strip for squaring up.

FOR 12" (30.5CM) BLOCKS

SS: short sashing strip (1½" × 12½" [3.8cm × 31.8cm])

Section A: 21" (53.3cm) subcut triangle

Section B: 14½" × 88" (36.8cm × 223.5cm)

TO MAKE B SECTION

Remove selvages from all four 14½" × wof (36.8cm × wof) strips. Sew two 14½" × wof (36.8cm × wof) strips together to make one 14½" × 88" (36.8cm × 223.5cm) strip. Repeat to yield two 14½" × 88" (36.8cm × 223.5cm) strips. Don't worry if your strips are longer than the pieced block strips. We need excess on both ends of the strip for squaring up.

Section C: 1½" × 110" (3.8cm × 279.4cm)

TO MAKE C SECTION

Remove selvages from three 1½" × wof (3.8cm × wof) strips. Sew the strips together to make one 1½" × 110" (3.8cm × 279.4cm) strip. Again, we need excess on both ends of the strip for squaring up.

Assemble the Quilt Top

Now that your sampler blocks, setting triangles and sashing strips are complete, it's time to play with layout. The block placement you choose can give the quilt its own personality. I encourage you to lay out the blocks in an arrangement that pleases your eye.

Because these blocks were made in inverse pairs, you can balance them within the block layout. In the sample, I placed blocks with heavier color concentrations in the small diagonal rows that contain only two blocks. This left many of the traditional, or white background, blocks to arrange in the center diagonal of the quilt. This is just one example. Play with it and try different arrangements.

As always, take a picture of each variation to help you decide, and once you're happy with your result, save that image. You may need it down the road to help you remember where your blocks go.

1 Lay out the assembled blocks, short sashing strips (SS), corners (A sections) and long sashing strips (B and C sections) in diagonal rows, following the Quilt Assembly Diagram.

2 Sew together the blocks and short sashing strips in each diagonal row. Press the seams toward the sashing strips.

3 Prior to joining the rows to make the quilt top, press a crease in each row to mark the center line (shown by the dotted line in the Quilt Assembly Diagram).

4 Join the rows to make the quilt top, aligning the center lines. Start with the middle rows and work outward. Make sure to align blocks across from each other for the 2 diagonal strips in the center of the quilt. Press toward the sashing strip.

5 Square up the quilt by trimming the extra sashing from sections A, B and C. I find that a large square ruler (20″ [50.8cm]) helps with this process.

Quilt Assembly Diagram

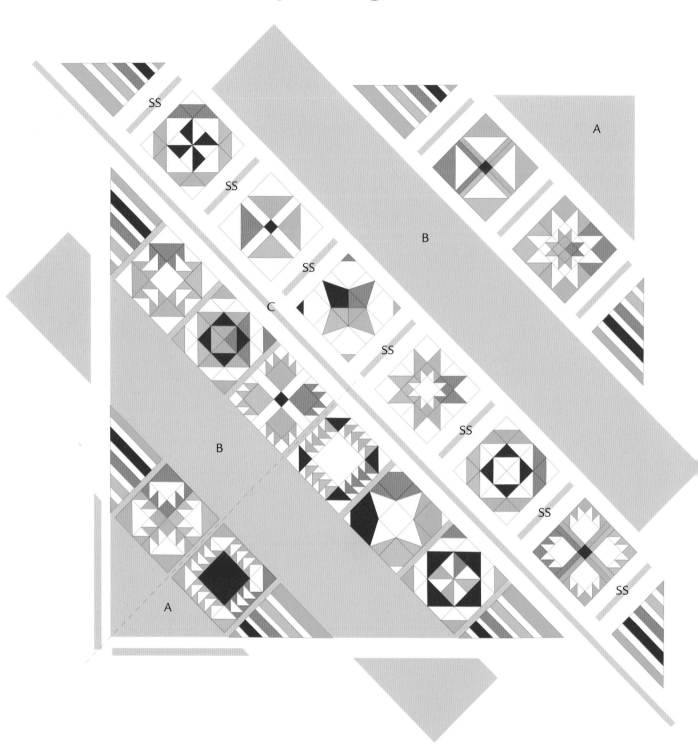

Prepare the Quilt for Finishing

THE 3 B'S: BATTING, BACKING AND BINDING

I like to have at least an extra 4" (10.2cm) on all four sides of a quilt for the batting and backing. This ensures that there is enough overlap to attach the quilt to the long-arm frame if you are sending your quilt out to a long-arm quilter or are long-arm quilting the quilt yourself. If you are quilting your own quilt on your home machine, you may not need as much overlap.

Backing

LAP QUILT (56½" [143.5M] SQUARE): Remove the selvages from the fabric and cut the total backing yardage in half lengthwise. Your 2 sections will be approximately 44" × 66" (111.8cm × 167.6cm). Cut 1 of the 2 sections to 22" × 66" (55.9cm × 167.6cm), then sew the 2 sections together along the 66" (167.6cm) side using a ½" (1.3cm) seam allowance. The backing should measure 66" × 65" (167.6cm × 165.1cm) (Figure 1).

TWIN QUILT (73½" [186.7CM] SQUARE): Remove the selvages from the fabric and cut the total backing yardage in half lengthwise. Your 2 sections will be approximately 44" × 83" (111.8cm × 210.8cm). Sew the 2 sections together along the 83" (210.8cm) side. The backing should measure 87" × 83" (221cm × 210.8cm) (Figure 2).

SCRAPPY BACK

These instructions assume your quilt back is made of one fabric, but feel free to use several and make it scrappy. Simply use the provided measurements as a guide for the finished dimensions of your back.

Batting

Cut the batting to the same size as the backing fabric.

Binding

LAP QUILT (56½" [143.5CM] SQUARE): From ½ yard (0.5m), cut seven 2½" (6.4cm) wide strips for double-fold straight-grain continuous binding. See the Binding tutorial in Chapter 4 for details.

TWIN QUILT (73½" [186.7CM] SQUARE): From ⅝ yard (0.6m), cut eight 2½" (6.4cm) wide strips for double-fold straight-grain continuous binding. See the Binding tutorial in Chapter 4 for details.

Vice Versa Sampler Backing

Lap (Figure 1)

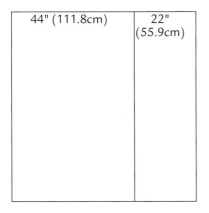

44" (111.8cm)   22" (55.9cm)

66" (167.6cm)

Twin (Figure 2)

44" (111.8cm)   44" (111.8cm)

83" (210.8cm)

Quilting Suggestions

Quilting a quilt like the **VICE VERSA SAMPLER** can be a little intimidating for some. In addition to the quilt blocks arranged on the diagonal of the quilt, there are some large negative space areas, too. These areas challenge us to think outside the box.

There are many quilting options to consider. Will you quilt one design edge to edge? Will you quilt the blocks independently of the negative space? Once you know how you'd like to quilt those areas, the most important question has been answered.

EDGE TO EDGE

I believe that any edge-to-edge design would look great on this quilt. Stipple, paisley, pebbles, crosshatching and other straight-line quilting ideas are all doable on your home machine.

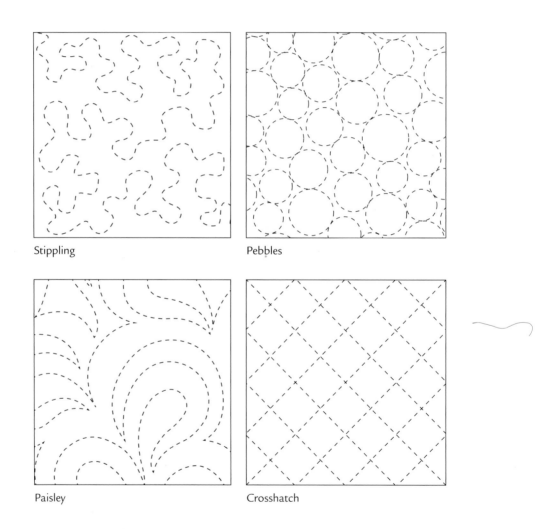

Stippling

Pebbles

Paisley

Crosshatch

FREE MOTION

Sampler quilts provide the perfect canvas for practicing different free-motion skills within each block. This time, think about quilting each block differently to perfect your skills or try new things. Before you begin, stitch in the ditch around each individual block. This will create a frame for you to work within. Then let your imagination soar!

Double Loop

Straight lines and stippling

Fingerlings, pebbles and boxed echo

Pebbles and scallops

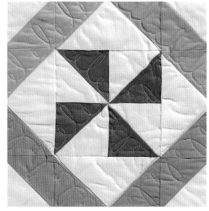

Loop-de-loops

Chrysanthemum

Original **VICE VERSA SAMPLER** by AnneMarie Chany.

VICE VERSA SAMPLER alternate colorway with wavy edge-to-edge quilting by Cristin Wilson.

Chapter 3

BONFIRE SAMPLER

The BONFIRE SAMPLER is a modern sampler that features some specialty blocks. The block patterns in this sampler introduce curves and string blocks as components of the overall block design. It's fun to add these elements to the sampler blocks as a little something unusual. Isn't it exciting to add these techniques to traditional blocks? Make it scrappy by using different fabrics within the blocks. Try using up your scraps where you can. String blocks are a great place for these.

The large Half-Square Triangles set up the overall look of the quilt, loosely based on the Bear's Paw block. To make this fun quilt, you will need sixteen quilt blocks. There are six new block patterns in this chapter. Making two of each block as sisters will give you twelve blocks. Choose two of your own favorite blocks from the previous chapters to make four more blocks to yield the sixteen needed.

Finished sizes:	Lap—64" (162.6cm) square (9" [22.9cm] finished blocks)
	Large Twin—82" (208.3cm) square (12" [30.5cm] finished blocks)
Number of blocks:	16 (make all 6 Chapter 3 patterns and choose 2 block patterns from Chapter 1 or Chapter 2)
Skill level:	Intermediate

◄ **BONFIRE SAMPLER,** designed and pieced by AnneMarie Chany. Quilted by Kathy Balmert.

Materials

Fabric estimates are based on yardage with 42" (106.7cm) of usable fabric. Fat quarters are 18" × 22" (45.7cm × 55.9cm); fat eighths are 9" × 22" (22.9cm × 55.9cm).

LAP—64" (162.6CM) SQUARE (9" [22.9CM] FINISHED BLOCKS)

½ yard (0.5m) total of each of 5 colors (aqua, purple, gold, orange and red) (for Fabrics B, C, D, E and F)

2 yards (1.8m) of linen in natural

1½ yards (1.4m) of a white solid

½ yard (0.5m) each of red and orange prints (fabrics for large setting Half-Square Triangles)

⅝ yard (0.6m) of binding fabric

4 yards (3.7m) for pieced backing

Batting 72" (182.9cm) square

LARGE TWIN—82" (208.3CM) (12" [30.5CM] FINISHED BLOCKS)

½ yard (0.5m) total each of 5 colors (aqua, purple, gold, orange and red) (for B, C, D, E and F)

3 yards (2.7m) of linen in natural

2 yards (1.8m) of white solid

¾ yard (0.7m) each of red and orange prints (fabrics for large setting Half-Square Triangles)

⅝ yard (0.6m) of binding fabric

7½ yards (6.9cm) for pieced backing

Batting 90" (228.6cm) square

SCRAPPY LOOK

Use scraps or fat eighths to create a scrappy look for the sampler blocks.

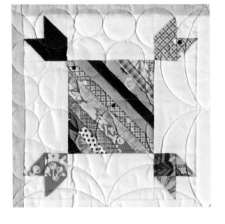

CUTTING INSTRUCTIONS FOR SASHING AND NEGATIVE SPACE

Cut large background pieces and sashing strips before you begin working through the blocks. Label the cuts with the appropriate letter in brackets, such as [A] and [B], to help you identify them when laying out the quilt top. Set these aside until you have completed all blocks for the quilt.

FOR 9" (22.9CM) BLOCKS

From linen, cut
Twenty 1½" × 9½" (3.8cm × 24.1cm) rectangles (A)

Two 1½" × 39½" (3.8cm × 100.3cm) rectangles (B)

Two 1½" × 41½" (3.8cm × 105.4cm) rectangles (C)

Four 9½" (24.1cm) squares (D)

Eight 10¼" (26cm) squares (E)

Two 3" × 59½" (7.6cm × 151.1cm) rectangles (border 1)

Two 3" × 64½" (7.6cm × 163.8cm) rectangles (border 2)

From white solid, cut
Twelve 1½" × 9½" (3.8cm × 24.1cm) rectangles (F)

Three 1½" × 39½" (3.8cm × 100.3cm) rectangles (G)

From orange print, cut
Four 10¼" (26cm) squares (H)

From red print, cut
Four 10¼" (26cm) squares (I)

FOR 12" (30.5CM) BLOCKS

From linen, cut
Twenty 1½" × 12½" (3.8cm × 31.8cm) rectangles (A)

Two 1½" × 51½" (3.8cm × 130.8cm) rectangles (B)

Two 1½" × 53½" (3.8cm × 135.9cm) rectangles (C)

Four 12½" (31.8cm) squares (D)

Eight 13¼" (33.7cm) squares (E)

Two 3" × 77½" (7.6cm × 196.9cm) rectangles (border 1)

Two 3" × 82½" (7.6cm × 209.6cm) rectangles (border 2)

From white solid, cut
Twelve 1½" × 12½" (3.8cm × 31.8cm) rectangles (F)

Three 1½" × 51½" (3.8cm × 130.8cm) rectangles (G)

From orange print, cut
Four 13¼" (33.7cm) squares (H)

From red print, cut
Four 13¼" (33.7cm) squares (I)

PIECING EXTRA-LONG STRIPS

Note that some of the sashing strips are very long and will require cutting a few width-of-fabric strips and piecing them together to get the total strip length.

For example, to make the 3" × 59½" (7.6cm × 151.1cm) strips, cut three 3" × wof (7.6cm × wof) strips and use those to make two 3" × 59½" (7.6cm × 151.1cm) strips.

Moon & Star

The Moon & Star block is a great block to begin with if you're new to curves. You will only need to sew four curves, which create a circle inside a star. Block no. 1 and Block no. 2 show ways to play with color placement.

Moon & Star Block no. 1

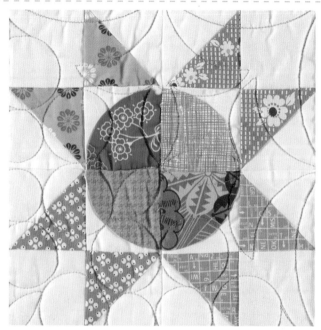

Moon & Star Block no. 2

CUTTING INSTRUCTIONS

Fabric A is the background fabric. Fabrics B, D, E and F are chosen from various fat eighths or scraps.

Moon & Star templates are located on pages 92 and 93.

FOR 9" (22.9CM) BLOCKS

From Fabric A, cut

Four 3½" (8.9cm) squares (large)

Four 2¾" (7cm) squares

Four of Template J

From each of Fabrics B, D, E and F, cut

One 3½" (8.9cm) square

One of Template K

FOR 12" (30.5CM) BLOCKS

From Fabric A, cut

Four 4¼" (10.8cm) squares (large)

Four 3½" (8.9cm) squares

Four of Template J

From each of Fabrics B, D, E and F, cut

One 4¼" (10.8cm) squares

One of Template K

PIECING INSTRUCTIONS

1 Make Half-Square Triangle (HST) units with the large Fabric A squares and Fabric B, Fabric D, Fabric E and Fabric F squares, respectively. Make 8 total HST units. See the Half-Square Triangle tutorial in Chapter 4 for details on making HSTs and squaring up. See the HSTs Yield table for quantities.

The HSTs should be trimmed to the following dimensions:
- ▶ 9″ (22.9cm) blocks: 2¾″ (7cm), unfinished
- ▶ 12″ (30.5cm) blocks: 3½″ (8.9cm), unfinished

HSTs Yield:
- ▶ 2 HSTs with Fabrics A/B
- ▶ 2 HSTs with Fabrics A/D
- ▶ 2 HSTs with Fabrics A/E
- ▶ 2 HSTs with Fabrics A/F

2 Make curved units, pairing Fabric A Template J pieces with Fabric B, Fabric D, Fabric E and Fabric F Template K pieces. Make 4 total curved units (Figure 1). See the Curves tutorial in Chapter 4 for details on sewing curves and squaring up.

The curved units should be squared to the following dimensions:
- ▶ 9″ (22.9cm) blocks: 2¾″ (7cm), unfinished
- ▶ 12″ (30.5cm) blocks: 3½″ (8.9cm), unfinished

3 Lay out the HST units, the curved units and the remaining 4 Fabric A squares (Figure 2).

4 Sew the units together to make 4 rows (Figure 3).

5 Sew the 4 rows together to complete the block (Figure 4).

6 Make 2 blocks for the **BONFIRE SAMPLER** quilt.

Figure 1

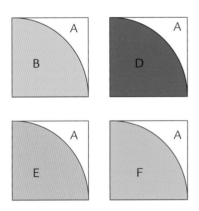

Figure 2

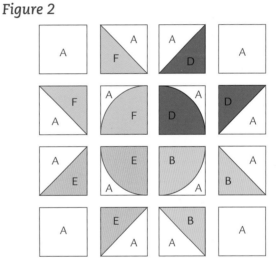

Figure 3

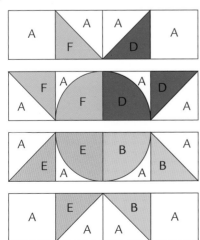

Figure 4

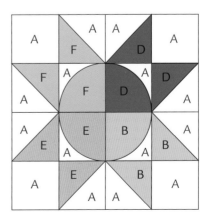

Button

The Button block is another way to make cute curves without having to rely on the Drunkard's Path look. Again, only four curves create a unique block.

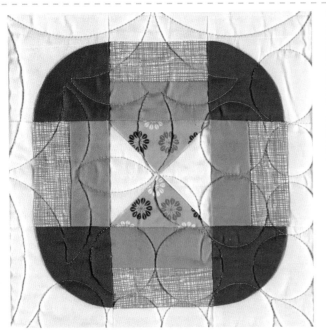

Button Block no. 1

Button Block no. 2

CUTTING INSTRUCTIONS

Fabric A is the background fabric. Fabric B–Fabric F are chosen from various fat eighths or scraps.

Button templates are located on pages 92 and 93.

FOR 9" (22.9CM) BLOCKS

From Fabric A, cut
Four 1¼" × 3½" (3.2cm × 8.9cm) rectangles

4 of Template L

One 5" (12.7cm) square

From each of Fabrics B and C, cut
Four 1⅝" × 3½" (4.1cm × 8.9cm) rectangles

From Fabric E, cut
4 of Template K

From Fabric F, cut
One 5" (12.7cm) square

FOR 12" (30.5CM) BLOCKS

From Fabric A, cut
Four 1½" × 4½" (3.2cm × 11.4cm) rectangles

4 of Template L

One 6" (15.2cm) square

From each of Fabrics B and C, cut
Four 2" × 4½" (5.1cm × 11.4cm) rectangles

From Fabric E, cut
4 of Template K

From Fabric F, cut
One 6" (15.2cm) square

PIECING INSTRUCTIONS

1 Make Hourglass units with Fabric A and Fabric F. Use the Fabric A square and the Fabric F square to make 2 Hourglass units. See the Quarter-Square Triangle tutorial in Chapter 4 for details on making QSTs and squaring up. This will yield 2 Hourglass units, but you only need 1 for this block. You may use the second Hourglass unit in the center of the second Button block if you desire.

The Hourglass units should be squared to the following dimensions:
- ► 9″ (22.9cm) blocks: 3½″ (8.9cm), unfinished
- ► 12″ (30.5cm) blocks: 4½″ (11.4cm), unfinished

2 Make a strip unit. Lay out the Fabric A, Fabric B and Fabric C rectangles. Sew the rectangles together to make the strip unit (Figure 1). Make 4.

3 Make curved units pairing the Fabric A Template L pieces with the Fabric E Template K pieces (Figure 2). Make 4 total curved units. See the Curves tutorial in Chapter 4 for details on sewing curves and squaring up.

The curved units should be squared to the following dimensions:
- ► 9″ (22.9cm) blocks: 3½″ (8.9cm), unfinished
- ► 12″ (30.5cm) blocks: 4½″ (11.4cm), unfinished

4 Lay out the Hourglass unit, the strip units and the curved units (Figure 3).

5 Sew the units together to make 3 rows (Figure 4).

6 Sew the 3 rows together to complete the block (Figure 5).

7 Make 2 blocks for the **BONFIRE SAMPLER** quilt.

Figure 1

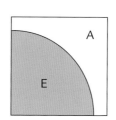

Make 4

Figure 2

Make 4

Figure 3

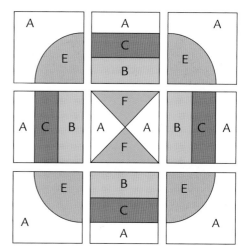

Figure 4

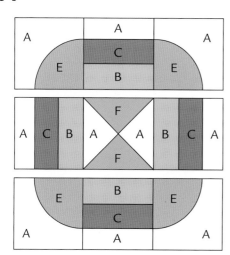

Figure 5

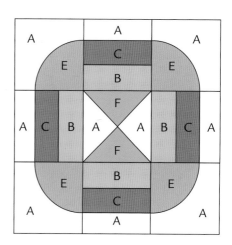

Time & Energy

The Time & Energy block combines two curves into a petal shape. Each petal surrounds a pinwheel in the center of the blocks. With eight curves to sew, this is a challenging curve block. Take your time and only work on one curve at a time. You'll be happy you did when this beautiful block is done.

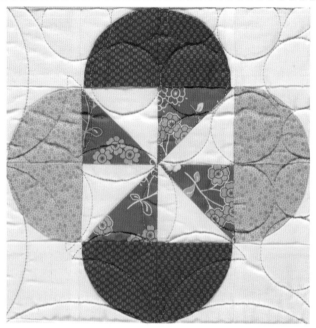

Time & Energy Block no. 1

Time & Energy Block no. 2

CUTTING INSTRUCTIONS

Fabric A is the background fabric. Fabrics B, D and F are chosen from various fat eighths or scraps.

Time & Energy templates are located on pages 92 and 93.

FOR 9" (22.9CM) BLOCKS

From Fabric A, cut
Four 2¾" (7cm) squares

Two 3½" (8.9cm) squares (large)

8 of Template J

From Fabric B, cut
4 of Template K

From Fabric D, cut
4 of Template K

From Fabric F, cut
Two 3½" (8.9cm) squares

FOR 12" (30.5CM) BLOCKS

From Fabric A, cut
Four 3½" (8.9cm) squares

Two 4¼" (10.8cm) squares (large)

8 of Template J

From Fabric B, cut
4 of Template K

From Fabric D, cut
4 of Template K

From Fabric F, cut
Two 4¼" (10.8cm) squares

PIECING INSTRUCTIONS

1 Make Half-Square Triangle (HST) units with Fabric A and Fabric F. Use the large Fabric A squares and the Fabric F squares to make 4 total HST units. See the Half-Square Triangle tutorial in Chapter 4 for details on making HSTs and squaring up.

The HSTs should be squared to the following dimensions:
- 9″ (22.9cm) blocks: 2¾″ (7cm), unfinished
- 12″ (30.5cm) blocks: 3½″ (8.9cm), unfinished

2 Make curved units pairing Fabric A Template J pieces with Fabric B and Fabric D Template K pieces. Make 8 total curved units (Figure 1). See the Curves tutorial in Chapter 4 for details on sewing curves and squaring up.

The curved units should be squared to the following dimensions:
- 9″ (22.9cm) blocks: 2¾″ (7cm), unfinished
- 12″ (30.5cm) blocks: 3½″ (8.9cm), unfinished

3 Lay out the HST units, remaining Fabric A squares and curved units (Figure 2).

4 Sew the units together into 4 rows (Figure 3).

5 Sew the 4 rows together to complete the block (Figure 4).

6 Make 2 blocks for the **BONFIRE SAMPLER** quilt.

Figure 1

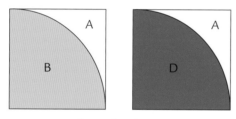

Make 4 of each variant

Figure 2

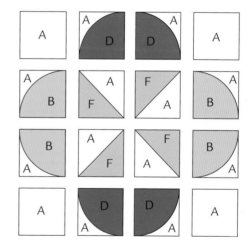

Figure 3

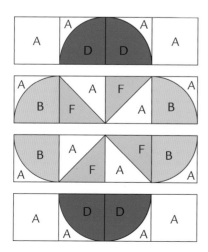

Figure 4

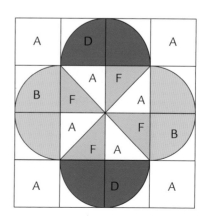

Templates

9" (22.9CM) CURVED TEMPLATES FOR MOON & STAR, BUTTON AND TIME & ENERGY BLOCKS

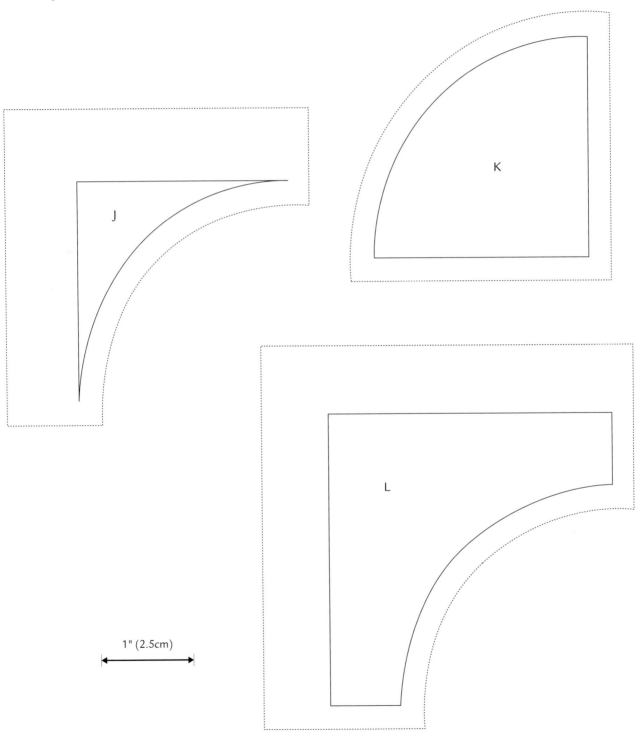

1" (2.5cm)

12" (30.5CM) CURVED TEMPLATES FOR MOON & STAR, BUTTON AND TIME & ENERGY BLOCKS

J

L

K

1" (2.5cm)

Box & Star Frame

String blocks are fun to make, but have you used them as a component within another block? I love to take special techniques and incorporate them as a part of other blocks. Strings take the center stage in this Box & Star Frame block.

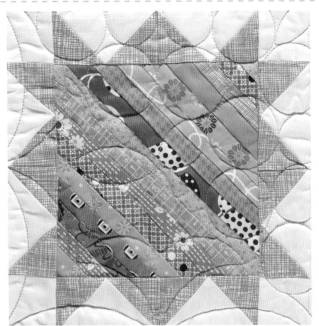

Box & Star Frame Block no. 1

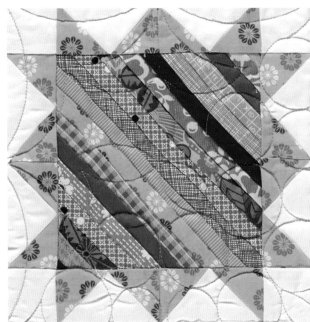

Box & Star Frame Block no. 2

CUTTING INSTRUCTIONS

Fabric A is the background fabric. Fabric B–Fabric F are chosen from various fat eighths and scraps.

FOR 9" (22.9CM) BLOCKS

From Fabric A, cut
Four 2" (5.1cm) squares

Two 4¼" (10.1cm) squares (large)

From Fabric C, cut
Eight 2⅜" (6cm) squares

From each of Fabrics B, C, D, E and F, cut
Various 1" (2.5cm) strips for strings

Additional supply:
Cut a piece of paper to 6½" (16.5cm) square

FOR 12" (30.5CM) BLOCKS

From Fabric A, cut
Four 2½" (6.4cm) squares

Two 5¼" (13.3cm) squares (large)

From Fabric C, cut
Eight 2⅞" (7.3cm) squares

From each of Fabrics B, C, D, E and F, cut
Various 1" (2.5cm) strips for strings

Additional supply:
Cut a piece of paper to 8½" (21.6cm) square

PIECING INSTRUCTIONS

1 **MAKE NO-WASTE FLYING GEESE.** Use 1 large Fabric A square and 4 Fabric C squares to make 4 No-Waste Flying Geese units. Make 8 total Flying Geese units. See the No-Waste Flying Geese tutorial in Chapter 4 for details on making Flying Geese 4 at a time.

The Flying Geese should measure the following dimensions:
- ▸ 9″ (22.9cm) blocks: 2″ × 3½″ (5.1cm × 8.9cm), unfinished
- ▸ 12″ (30.5cm) blocks: 2½″ × 4½″ (6.4cm × 11.45cm), unfinished

2 **MAKE A STRING BLOCK.** Using the piece of paper cut to size and the various 1″ (2.5cm) strips of Fabric B, Fabric C, Fabric D, Fabric E and Fabric F, make 1 string block. See the String block tutorial in Chapter 4 for details on making String blocks and squaring up.

The String block should measure the following dimensions:
- ▸ 9″ (22.9cm) blocks: 6½″ (16.5cm), unfinished
- ▸ 12″ (30.5cm) blocks: 8½″ (21.6cm), unfinished

3 Lay out the 8 Flying Geese units, the String block and the remaining 4 Fabric A squares (Figure 1).

4 Sew the 2 Flying Geese on the left of the String block together. Repeat with the 2 Flying Geese on the right of the String block. Repeat with the Flying Geese on the top and bottom of the String block (Figure 2).

5 Sew the units together into 3 rows (Figure 3).

6 Sew the 3 rows together to complete the block (Figure 4).

7 Make 2 blocks for the **BONFIRE SAMPLER** quilt.

Figure 1

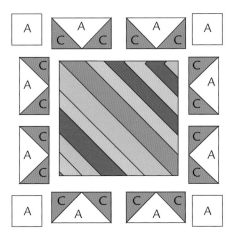

Figure 2

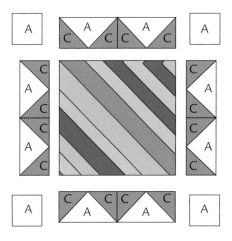

Figure 3

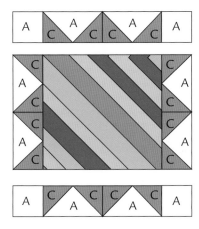

Figure 4

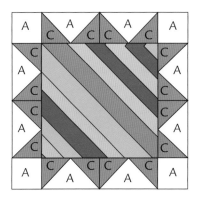

Tulip Lady Fingers

Four petals flank the String block in our version of Tulip Lady Fingers. It's a cute variation that adds some pizzazz to this simple block. This block is playful when each petal is a different color.

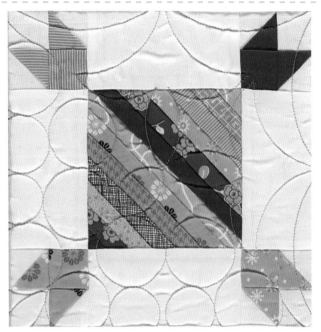

Tulip Lady Fingers Block no. 1

Tulip Lady Fingers Block no. 2

CUTTING INSTRUCTIONS

Fabric A is the background fabric. Fabric B–Fabric F are chosen from various fat eighths and scraps.

FOR 9" (22.9CM) BLOCKS

From Fabric A, cut

Four 1⅝" (4.1cm) squares (small)

Four 2⅜" (6cm) squares (large)

Four 2¾" × 5" (7cm × 12.7cm) rectangles

From each of Fabrics C, D, E and F, cut

One 1⅝" (4.1cm) square (small)

One 2⅜" (6cm) square (large)

From each of Fabrics B, C, D, E and F, cut

Various 1" (2.5cm) strips for strings

Additional Supply:

Cut a piece of paper to 5" (12.7cm) square

FOR 12" (30.5CM) BLOCKS

From Fabric A, cut

Four 2" (5.1cm) squares (small)

Four 2¾" (7cm) squares (large)

Four 3½" × 6½" (8.9cm × 16.5cm) rectangles

From each of Fabrics C, D, E and F, cut

One 2" (5.1cm) square (small)

One 2¾" (7cm) square (large)

From each of Fabrics B, C, D, E and F, cut

Various 1" (2.5cm) strips for strings

Additional Supply:

Cut a piece of paper to 6½" (16.5cm) square

PIECING INSTRUCTIONS

1 Make Half-Square Triangle (HST) units with Fabric A and Fabric C, Fabric D, Fabric E and Fabric F. Use the large Fabric A squares and the large Fabric C, Fabric D, Fabric E and Fabric F squares to make 8 total HST units. See the Half-Square Triangle tutorial in Chapter 4 for details on making HSTs and squaring up. See the HSTs Yield table for quantities.

The HSTs should be trimmed to the following dimensions:
- ▶ 9″ (22.9cm) blocks: 1⅝″ (4.1cm), unfinished
- ▶ 12″ (30.5cm) blocks: 2″ (5.1cm), unfinished

HSTs Yield:
- ▶ 2 HSTs with Fabrics A/C
- ▶ 2 HSTs with Fabrics A/D
- ▶ 2 HSTs with Fabrics A/E
- ▶ 2 HSTs with Fabrics A/F

2 **MAKE STRING BLOCK.** Using the piece of paper cut to size and the various 1″ (2.5cm) strips of Fabric B, Fabric C, Fabric D, Fabric E and Fabric F, make 1 String block. See the String block tutorial in Chapter 4 for details on making String blocks and squaring up.

The String block should measure the following dimensions:
- ▶ 9″ (22.9cm) blocks: 5″ (12.7cm), unfinished
- ▶ 12″ (30.5cm) blocks: 6½″ (16.5cm), unfinished

3 Lay out the HST units, the small Fabric A, Fabric C, Fabric D, Fabric E and Fabric F squares, the String block and the Fabric A rectangles (Figure 1).

4 **ASSEMBLE THE PETALS.** Sew the 2 Fabric A/C HSTs, 1 small Fabric A square and 1 small Fabric C square together into 2 rows. Then sew the 2 rows together to complete the petal unit (Figure 2). Repeat this step for the 3 remaining petals.

The Petal blocks should measure the following dimensions:
- ▶ 9″ (22.9cm) blocks: 2¾″ (7cm), unfinished
- ▶ 12″ (30.5cm) blocks: 3½″ (8.9cm), unfinished

5 Sew the units together into 3 rows (Figure 3).

6 Sew the 3 rows together to complete the block (Figure 4).

7 Make 2 blocks for the **BONFIRE SAMPLER** quilt.

Figure 1

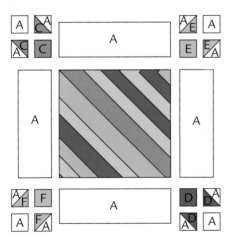

Figure 2

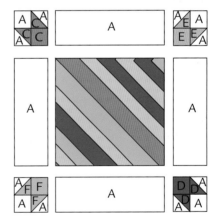

Figure 3

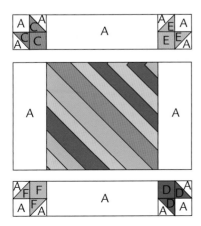

Figure 4

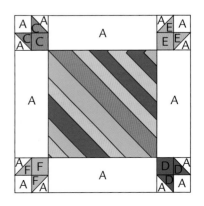

Friendship Star

Jazz up this classic block and give it a fresh look by featuring strings in the star points.

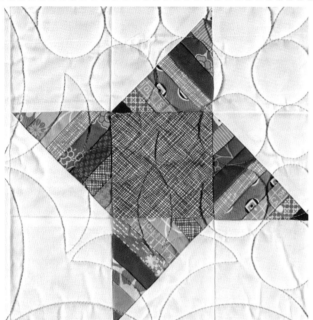

Friendship Star Block no. 1

Friendship Star Block no. 2

CUTTING INSTRUCTIONS

Fabric A is the background fabric. Fabric B–Fabric F are chosen from various fat eighths or scraps.

FOR 9" (22.9CM) BLOCKS

From Fabric A, cut
Four 3½" (8.9cm) squares

Two 4¼" (10.8cm) squares (large)

From Fabric E, cut
One 3½" (8.9cm) square

From each of Fabrics B, C, D, E and F, cut
Various 1" (2.5cm) strips for strings

Additional Supply:
Cut a piece of paper into two 4¼" (10.8cm) squares

FOR 12" (30.5CM) BLOCKS

From Fabric A, cut
Four 4½" (11.4cm) squares

Two 5¼" (13.3cm) squares (large)

From Fabric E, cut
One 4½" (11.4cm) square

From each of Fabrics B, C, D, E and F, cut
Various 1" (2.5cm) strips for strings

Additional Supply:
Cut a piece of paper into two 5¼" (13.3cm) squares

PIECING INSTRUCTIONS

1 Using the pieces of paper cut to size and the various 1″ (2.5cm) strips of Fabric B, Fabric C, Fabric D, Fabric E and Fabric F, make 2 String blocks. See the String block tutorial in Chapter 4 for details on making string blocks and squaring up.

The String blocks should measure the following dimensions:
- ▸ 9″ blocks: 4¼″ (10.8cm), unfinished
- ▸ 12″ blocks: 5¼″ (13.3cm), unfinished

2 Make Half-Square Triangle (HST) units with the large Fabric A squares and String blocks. Use the 2 large Fabric A squares and the 2 String blocks to make 4 total HST units. Be sure to place the diagonal sewing/cutting line perpendicular to the strings. See the Half-Square Triangle tutorial in Chapter 4 for details on making HSTs and squaring up.

The HSTs should be squared to the following dimensions:
- ▸ 9″ (22.9cm) blocks: 3½″ (8.9cm), unfinished
- ▸ 12″ (30.5cm) blocks: 4½″ (11.4cm), unfinished

3 Lay out the HST units, the remaining Fabric A squares and Fabric E square (Figure 1).

4 Sew the units together into 3 rows (Figure 2).

5 Sew the 3 rows together to complete the block (Figure 3).

6 Make 2 blocks for the **BONFIRE SAMPLER** quilt.

Figure 1

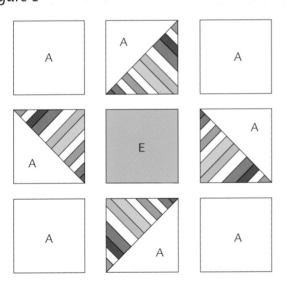

Figure 2

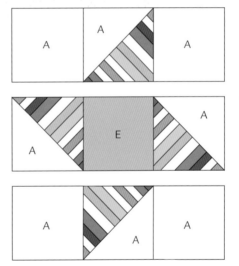

Figure 3

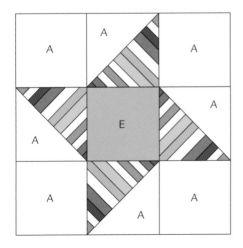

Assemble the Quilt Top

It's time to have fun laying out the blocks in this sampler. You have made two of each block, and there are many possible layouts, so be sure to play around with it a bit. You may choose a random placement, or you may balance the blocks in opposing quadrants. Try different arrangements. Try rotating some blocks. As always, take a picture of each variation to help you decide. Once you have your final arrangement, take a picture of that as well so you don't forget the order of the blocks.

See the Cutting Instructions for Sashing and Negative Space on page 85 for cutting and labeling your sashing.

Quilt Assembly Diagrams

1 Make Half-Square Triangle (HST) units with pieces E/H and E/I. Use the Linen E squares and the Orange H squares to make 8 total E/H HST units, then use the Linen E squares and the Red I squares to make 8 total E/I HST units. See the Half-Square Triangle tutorial in Chapter 4 for details on making HSTs and squaring up.

The HSTs should be squared to the following dimensions:
- 9″ (22.9cm) blocks: 9½″ (24.1cm), unfinished
- 12″ (30.5cm) blocks: 12½″ (31.8cm), unfinished

2 Lay out the assembled blocks, sashing strips A–G, the E/H and E/I HSTs and the border strips as shown in Figure 1.

3 Sew the sampler blocks into rows of 4, sewing sashing F strips in between each block. Sew the 4 rows together, sewing a sashing G strip in between each row (Figure 2).

4 Sew the linen C sashing to the left and right sides of the center unit, then sew the linen B sashing to the top and bottom of the center unit. Next sew 2 E/H HSTs, 2 E/I HSTs and 5 sashing A strips to make the left-hand column. Repeat to make the right-hand column (Figure 3).

Figure 1

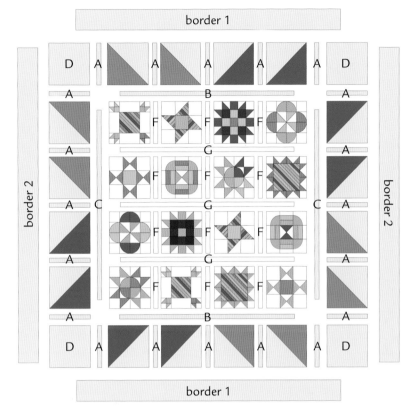

Figure 2

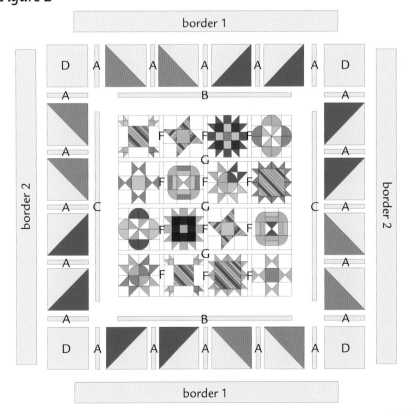

5 Next, sew 2 E/H HSTs, 2 E/I HSTs, 2 linen D squares and 5 sashing A strips to make the top row. Repeat to make the bottom row (Figure 3).

6 Sew the left- and right-hand HST columns to the center unit, then sew the top and bottom rows to the center unit (Figure 4).

7 Sew the border 1 strips to the top and bottom of the center unit. Lastly, sew the border 2 strips to the left and right side of the center unit to complete the quilt top (Figure 5).

Figure 4

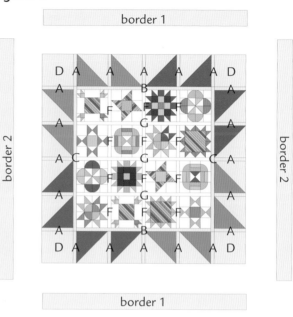

Figure 3

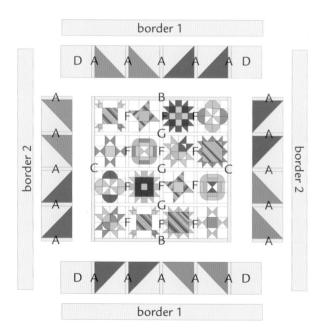

Figure 5

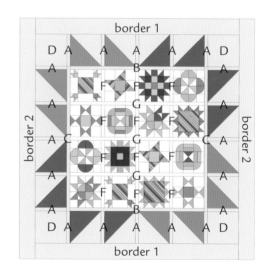

Prepare the Quilt for Finishing

THE 3 B'S: BATTING, BACKING AND BINDING

I like to have at least an extra 4" (10.2cm) on all four sides of a quilt for the batting and backing. This ensures that there is enough overlap to attach the quilt to the long-arm frame if you are sending your quilt out to a long-arm quilter or are long-arm quilting it yourself. If you are quilting your own quilt on your home machine, you may not need as much overlap.

Backing

LAP QUILT (64" [162.6CM] SQUARE): Remove the selvages from the fabric and cut the total backing yardage in half lengthwise. Your 2 sections will be approximately 44" × 72" (111.8cm × 182.9cm). Cut 1 of the 2 sections to 28" × 72" (71.1cm × 182.9cm), then sew the 2 sections together along the 72" (182.9cm) side using a ½" (1.3cm) seam allowance. The backing should measure 71" × 72" (180.3cm × 182.9cm) (Figure 1).

TWIN QUILT (82" [208.3CM] SQUARE): Remove the selvages from the fabric. Cut the backing into three 43" × 90" (109.2cm × 228.6cm) sections. Cut 1 of those 3 sections down to 6" × 90" (15.2cm × 228.6cm). Sew the 3 sections together along the 90" (228.6cm) side using a ½" (1.3cm) seam allowance. The backing should measure 90" (228.6cm) square (Figure 2).

WIDE BACKING FABRICS

There are some fabrics that come in wider widths to use for backing. For this larger quilt, you may be able to save money if you use a 90" (228.6cm) or 108" (274.3cm) wide backing fabric. You will need to buy 2½ yards (2.3m) of 90" (228.6cm) or 108" (274.3cm) wide fabric to make your backing at least 90" × 90" (228.6cm × 228.6cm) wide.

Batting

Cut the batting to the same size as the backing fabric.

Binding

LAP QUILT (64" [162.6CM] SQUARE): From ⅝ yard (0.6m), cut seven 2½" (6.4cm) wide strips for double-fold continuous straight-grain binding. See the Binding tutorial in Chapter 4 for details.

TWIN QUILT (82" [208.3CM] SQUARE): From ⅝ yard (0.6m), cut nine 2½" (6.4cm) wide strips for double-fold straight-grain continuous binding.

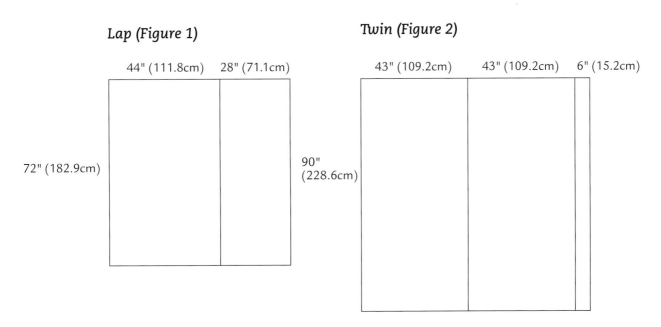

Lap (Figure 1)

44" (111.8cm) 28" (71.1cm)

72" (182.9cm)

Twin (Figure 2)

43" (109.2cm) 43" (109.2cm) 6" (15.2cm)

90" (228.6cm)

Quilting Suggestions

For the third quilt in this book, I try to offer a third approach to quilting modern quilts. In the **SISTERS' TEN SAMPLER**, an all-over edge-to-edge design was demonstrated. In the **VICE VERSA SAMPLER**, blocks were individually quilted. In the **BONFIRE SAMPLER**, there are certain areas of specialized quilting, with the majority of the quilt done in an all-over design. It is my hope that by demonstrating these three different approaches, it will help you to think outside the box when it comes time to quilt your own quilts. The modern aesthetics of these samplers give you a lot of freedom to quilt something unique.

For the center portion of the sampler, which showcases the sampler blocks, I chose an edge-to-edge design that is modern in feel. It contains a pattern of petals and circles that was quilted by a long-arm quilter.

The large Half-Square Triangles that frame the quilt contain straight lines that cut diagonally across the triangle. These lines draw attention to the star that frames the center work of the quilt.

Lastly, the negative space outside the large star is quilted with a stipple pattern. Think of different ways you can break up these three components of the quilt top to create an eye-catching design. There are many possibilities.

Petals and circles in the center space between blocks.

Diagonal lines quilted in the Half-Square Triangles and stippling in the negative space outside the star.

BONFIRE SAMPLER by AnneMarie Chany.

Chapter 4

TUTORIALS

SCANT RANT

To improve your piecing, one of the most important things you can do is test your ¼" (6mm) seam for accuracy. Don't make the same mistake I did. For years, I sewed with a true ¼" (6mm) seam. I never took the time to find the scant ¼" (6mm), and as a result, my seams and resulting block sizes were always a little off.

I didn't realize that the thread and seam take up some space in the measurement, which makes the block come up short. Spending just a few minutes to adjust your machine to a scant ¼" (6mm) will save you many headaches.

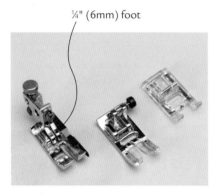

¼" (6mm) foot

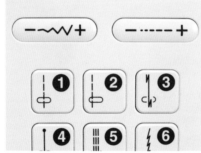

Presser foot

Sewing machines generally come with default generic presser feet. The zigzag foot and satin-stitch foot are used for most stitches and straight-line sewing. Some higher-end models may come with a ¼" (6mm) foot. The ¼" (6mm) foot is specifically for quilters trying to sew that perfect ¼" (6mm) seam. If you don't have a ¼" (6mm) foot already, I highly recommend getting one. The black guide on the right side of the foot helps position your fabric by butting the edges of the squares right up against the guide.

Adjustable Needle Position

Before you can find your scant ¼" (6mm) seam, you will need to determine whether your sewing machine has an adjustable needle position. Some basic machines do not have this feature. Higher-end models allow you to shift the needle to the left or right 1 millimeter at a time. Follow the appropriate guideline based on your machine type.

Fixed Needle Position

If the needle on your sewing machine is in a fixed position (meaning you cannot shift it right or left), an easy way to keep your scant ¼" (6mm) is to find where you need to sew to get your ¼" (6mm), then place a small piece of tape on the throat plate to serve as your guide.

Scant ¼" (6mm) vs. True ¼" (6mm)

Most of the time, the needle position will need to be adjusted from its default position to achieve the scant ¼" (6mm). Above, you can see that sewing the seam with the needle in its default position (right) results in a block that is slightly shy of the 2" (5.1cm) it's supposed to be. It may take a little time playing with the needle position to find where it hits exactly on 2" (5.1cm). After finding the correct position for the scant ¼" (6mm) seam, adjust your machine to that needle position every time you sew.

TEST: ADJUSTABLE-NEEDLE SEWING MACHINE

1 Cut two 1¼" × 2" (3.2cm × 5.1cm) rectangles. Sew along the 2" (5.1cm) length with right sides together, using the edge of the presser foot as your guide. Press the seam.

2 Measure the block to see if it's 2" (5.1cm) square.

3 If the width of the block is short, your needle will need to shift to the right.

4 If the width of the block is too long, your needle will need to shift to the left.

5 Shift the needle one or two notches at a time until you find the sweet spot where the block measures 2" (5.1cm).

TEST: FIXED-NEEDLE SEWING MACHINE

1 Cut two 1¼" × 2" (3.2cm × 5.1cm) rectangles. Sew along the 2" (5.1cm) length with right sides together, using the edge of the presser foot as your guide. Press the seam.

2 Measure the block to see if it's 2" (5.1cm) square.

3 If the width of the block is short, you will need to place a piece of tape slightly to the left of the presser-foot edge.

4 If the width of the block is too long, you will need to place a piece of tape slightly to the right of the presser-foot edge.

5 Continue shifting the tape a little at a time until you find the sweet spot where the block measures 2" (5.1cm).

Notice how much space is between the tape and the edge of the presser foot. This measurement may be just a few millimeters, but that dimension will add up to a larger amount with each seam you sew in the quilt.

After finding the correct location for the tape, line up your squares and/or rectangles to be sewn with the tape (not the edge of the presser foot) each time you need a scant ¼" (6mm).

PRESSING SEAMS

Does it make a difference if you press your seams open or to the side in your final block measurements? Because a scant ¼" (6mm) accounts for your thread and the pressed fold taking up some space in the measurement, the answer is yes. My recommendation is to find your scant ¼" (6mm) using the pressing method you use most. Or if you're into superhero precision, determine your scant ¼" (6mm) for both. As for me, I'm no superhero.

Half-Square Triangles

In this example, we begin with two 4¼" (13.3cm) squares. The HST will be squared up to an unfinished size of 3½" (8.9cm). All HSTs in this book are made using this method. The cuts are slightly large so there is room to square them up later. Squaring up all the HSTs will help improve your accuracy when piecing the blocks.

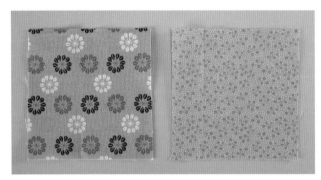

1 Cut 2 squares the same size, 1 from Fabric A and 1 from Fabric B.

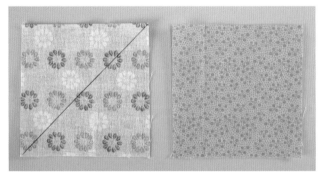

2 Draw a diagonal line on the wrong side of the Fabric A square.

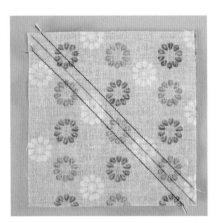

3 Layer the Fabric A square on top of the Fabric B square with right sides together. Sew the pair together, stitching ¼" (6mm) on each side of the drawn line.

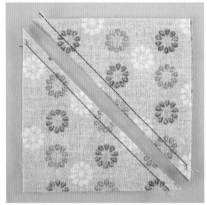

4 Cut the pair along the drawn line to make 2 Half-Square Triangle units.

HALF-SQUARE TRIANGLE EQUATION

CUT: 2 squares at Y+1¼" (3.2m) square
SQUARE UP: 2 HSTs Y+½" (1.3cm) square (unfinished size)
FINISHED SIZE: 2 HSTs Y" (Ycm) square

EXAMPLE:
CUT: 2 squares 5¼" (13.3cm) square
SQUARE UP: 2 HSTs 4½" (11.4cm) square
FINISHED SIZE: 2 HSTs 4" (10.2cm) square

Note: Y = Desired finished block size

5 Open the Half-Square Triangle blocks, pressing the seam allowances toward the darker fabric.

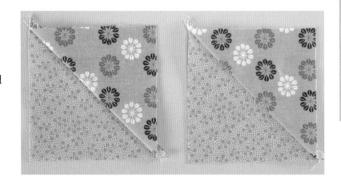

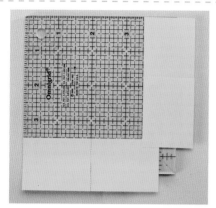

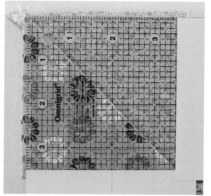

RIGHT-HANDED SQUARING

If you're right handed, simply reverse the sides you cut so that they're on the top and right side. Then rotate your piece so that you're cutting on the top and right again.

6 On a ruler, mark off the unfinished size to which the block needs to be trimmed. It helps to place sticky notes along the grid lines so you can see the appropriate size without getting confused. In this example, a 3½" (8.9cm) square is gridded off on the ruler.

7 Lay the diagonal of the ruler on top of the diagonal of the block seam. Make sure to center the marked-off section of the ruler over the block so there is a small amount of fabric to trim on all sides. Visually check that there is fabric overlap past your mark-offs on all 4 sides before proceeding to cut.

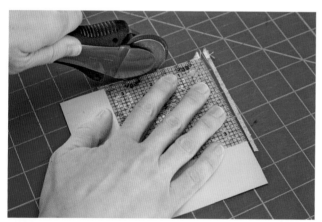

8 Use your rotary cutter to trim the excess on the top and left side first.

9 Lift the ruler off the block and turn it 180°. The 2 sides you just cut should be on the right and bottom. Trim the remaining 2 sides, which are now on the top and left. Be sure to align the ruler over the diagonal again and place the right and bottom edges of the block at the marked-off size on the ruler.

10 Your finished Half-Square Triangle.

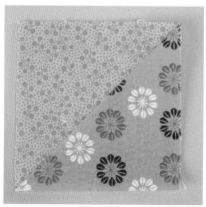

Quarter-Square Triangles

Quarter-Square Triangles take the basic Half-Square Triangle up a notch. It is exactly as it sounds. Four triangles make up one square. In some cases, we do have to cut the triangles and sew them back together. But there is a fancy way to sew these and avoid handling all those bias edges.

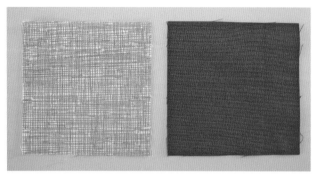

1 Cut 2 squares the same size, 1 from Fabric A and 1 from Fabric B. Draw a diagonal line on the wrong side of the Fabric A square.

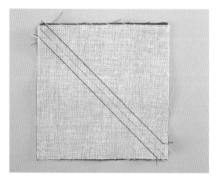

2 Layer the Fabric A square on top of the Fabric B square with right sides together. Sew the pair together, stitching ¼" (6mm) on each side of the drawn line.

3 Cut the pair apart along the drawn line using a rotary cutter.

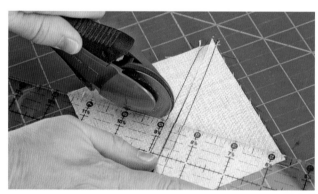

4 Without moving the blocks you just cut, place your ruler over the opposite diagonal and cut. There are now 4 triangle units. Each unit has 1 A triangle and 1 B triangle.

5 Press the seam allowances toward the darker fabric and match up pairs of triangles to form an Hourglass block.

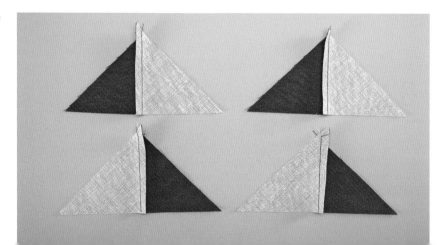

6 Pin the triangles in place and sew. Don't skip the pinning here! When sewing triangles with exposed bias edges, the simple act of pinning can prevent your triangles from becoming distorted.

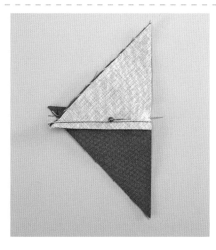

7 Press the block open.

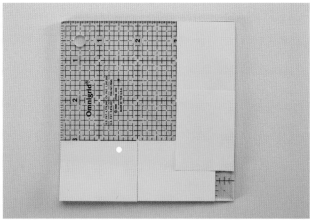

8 On your ruler, mark the unfinished size to which the blocks need to be trimmed. Place sticky notes on the grid lines at the appropriate size to prevent any confusion. In this example, a 3″ (7.6cm) square is blocked off on the ruler. Mark the center of the block on your ruler.

9 Lay the diagonal of the ruler on top of one of the diagonals of the Hourglass block. Make sure the center dot of the ruler is at the intersection of the block. Trim the excess fabric on all sides.

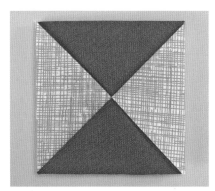

10 Your finished Quarter-Square Triangle, also called an Hourglass block.

QUARTER-SQUARE TRIANGLE EQUATION

CUT: 2 squares at Y+1½″ (3.8m) square
SQUARE UP: 2 QSTs Y+½″ (1.3cm) square (unfinished size)
FINISHED SIZE: 2 QSTs Y″ (Ycm)square

EXAMPLE:
CUT: 2 squares 5½″ (14cm) square
SQUARE UP: 2 QSTs 4½″ (11.5cm) square
FINISHED SIZE: 2 QSTs 4″ (10.2cm) square

Note: Y = Desired finished block size

Flying Geese

Flying Geese are fundamental quilt blocks used alone or as components of other blocks throughout quilting history. Use this block to build your repertoire of basic quilt blocks.

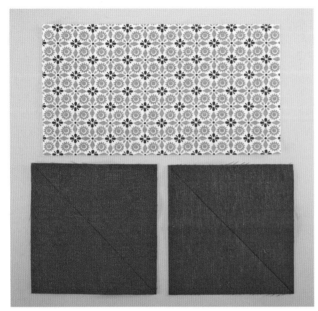

1 Cut 2 squares the same size and 1 rectangle with its length twice that of its width. Draw a diagonal line on the wrong side of the 2 squares.

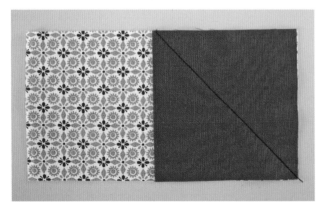

2 Lay 1 square right sides together on top of the rectangle with the diagonal running from the top left corner to the bottom right corner. Sew on the drawn line.

3 Trim the excess fabric by cutting ¼" (6mm) away from the stitching.

FLYING GEESE EQUATION

CUT SQUARES: Two Y+½" (1.3cm) squares

CUT RECTANGLE: 1 rectangle Y+½" (1.3cm) × 2Y+½"(1.3cm)

MAKES (UNFINISHED): 1 Flying Goose Y+½" × 2Y+½ (Y+1.3cm × 2Y+1.3cm)

FINISHED SIZE: 1 Flying Goose Y" × 2Y" (Ycm × 2Ycm)

EXAMPLE:

SQUARES: Two 4½" (11.4cm) squares

RECTANGLE: 1 rectangle 4½" × 8½" (11.4cm × 21.6cm)

MAKES (UNFINISHED): 1 Flying Goose 4½" × 8½" (11.4cm × 21.6cm)

FINISHED SIZE: 1 Flying Goose 4" × 8" (10.2cm × 20.3cm)

Note: Y = Desired finished block size.

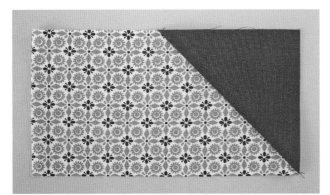

4 Open the sewn unit and press the seam allowances toward the darker fabric.

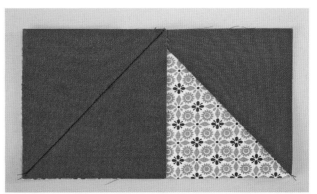

5 Place the second square on top of the unit from the previous step, right sides together with the diagonal running from the bottom left corner to the top right corner. Sew on the drawn line.

6 Trim the excess by cutting ¼″ (6mm) away from the stitching.

7 Press the second seam allowances toward the darker fabric to complete the Flying Geese unit.

Sometimes a Flying Geese unit can end up a little small when the triangles are flipped open and pressed. This is due to the space that the thread and fold take up. To make sure your units are not on the small side, stitch about a thread's width away from the drawn line toward the outside corner of the unit. When you flip the triangle open, there will be more fabric available for opening. Any excess can then be trimmed and squared if needed.

No-Waste Flying Geese

Sometimes you need a lot of Flying Geese units to make a quilt or quilt block. If you need a lot of Geese, there's a time- and fabric-saving method that allows you to make eight Flying Geese units at once. There is never enough time in the day, so this shortcut can be very helpful.

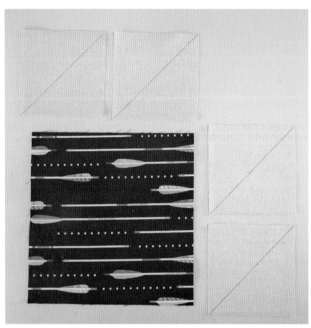

1 Use 1 large square and 4 small squares to make 4 Flying Geese units. Draw a diagonal line on the wrong side of the small squares.

NO-WASTE FLYING GEESE EQUATION

DESIRED FINISHED SIZE: 4 Flying Geese Y" × 2Y" (Ycm × 2Ycm)

MAKES (UNFINISHED): 4 Flying Geese Y+½" × 2Y+½" (Y+1.3cm × 2Y+1.3cm)

CUT: 1 large 2Y" + 1¼" (2Ycm + 3.2cm) square

CUT: 4 small Y" + ⅞" (Ycm + 2.2cm) square

EXAMPLE:

DESIRED FINISHED SIZE: 4 Flying Geese 4" × 8" (10.2cm × 20.3cm)

MAKES (UNFINISHED): 4 Flying Geese 4½" × 8½" (11.4cm × 21.6cm)

CUT: 1 large 9¼" (23.5cm) square

CUT: 4 small 4⅞" (12.4cm) squares

Note: Y = Desired finished block size

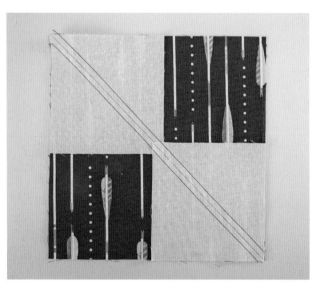

2 Layer 2 small squares on top of the large square with right sides together as shown. The small squares will overlap slightly. Sew the pairs together, stitching ¼" (6mm) on each side of the drawn line.

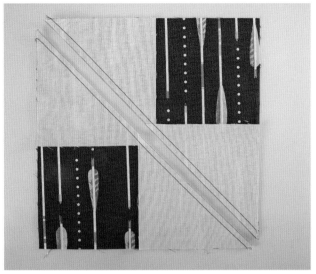

3 Cut the pair apart along the drawn line.

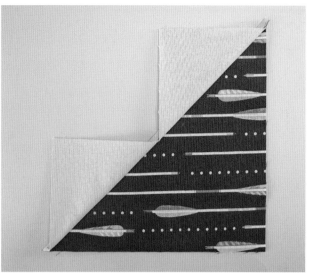

4 Press the units open. I recommend pressing toward the smaller triangle points to avoid distorting them.

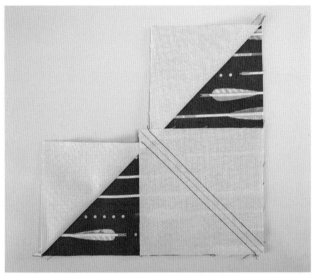

5 Place another small square on top of the unit from the previous step as shown. Sew the pairs together, stitching ¼" (6mm) on each side of the drawn line.

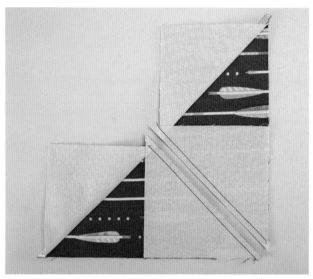

6 Cut the pair along the drawn line.

7 Press the seam allowances toward the triangle points to make 4 Flying Geese units. Repeat with the other half of the original square to make 2 more units.

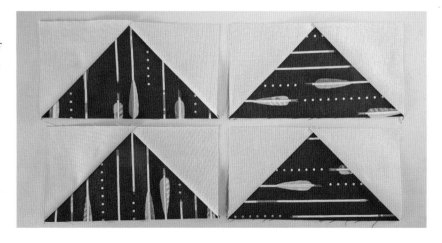

Curves

Curves are a wonderful way to add visual interest to a quilt. Don't worry . . . they're not as hard to make as they look. If you've never made a curved block before, try it with some scraps first to get a feel for it. Curved blocks are sometimes referred to as Drunkard's Path blocks.

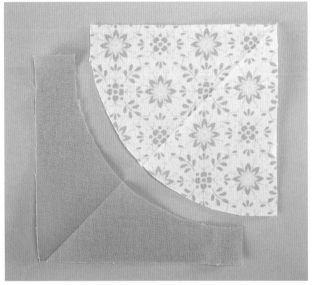

1 Find the center of all the Template J, K or L pieces (from pages 92 and 93) by folding the pieces in half and pressing to mark the center line.

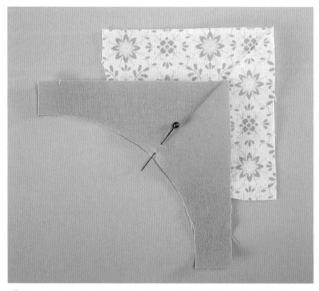

2 Lay 1 Template K right-side up. Place 1 Template J or L right-side down on top of Template K, aligning the center lines. Pin at the center.

3 Pin the edges of Template J or L to the curved edge of Template K. Work from the center outward. The number of pins you use is up to you. I prefer at least 3 pins. Sometimes it helps to make a very small clip in Template J or L to ease the fabric around the curve.

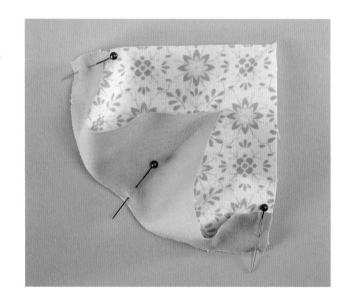

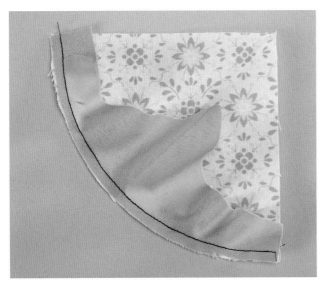

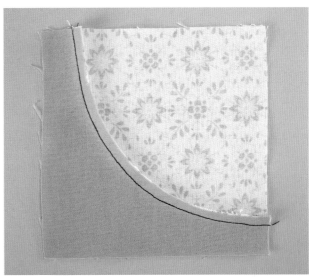

4 Sew the pieces together along the pinned curved edge. Sew slowly and ease in the fabric along the curve.

5 Press the seam allowance toward the curve, Template K.

¼" (6mm) ¼" (6mm)

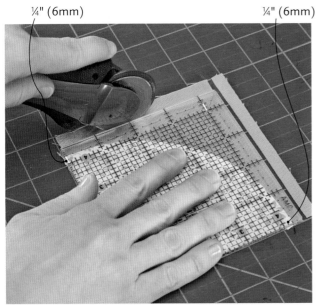

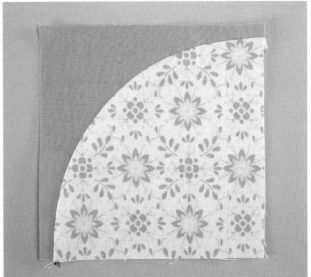

6 The Template J or L pieces are oversized to allow for squaring up after sewing, because it's easy for curve blocks to get distorted. To square up the blocks, place your ruler ¼" (6mm) away from the edge of the curve (indicated by the arrows). Trim the excess.

7 Your curve block is now complete.

Strings

Traditionally, String blocks are thought to be a standalone block. Using them as components of other quilt blocks, however, makes them more fun. You can use this technique to jazz up a lot of traditional quilt blocks.

Note: Adjust the stitch length of your machine to a very small stitch, such as 1.3, to help perforate the paper.

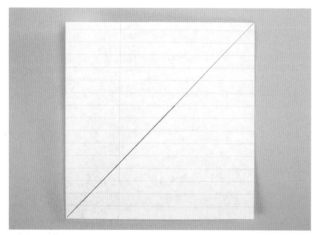

1 Cut computer or notebook paper down to the needed size, which includes ¼" (6mm) on all sides for seam allowances. Find the diagonal of the square by folding or marking the line.

2 The String blocks in this book are made from 1" × width-of-fabric (wof) (2.5cm × wof) strips or 1" (2.5cm) wide scraps. The strings are not precut to given lengths to allow you some creative freedom. Choose each string color as you desire. Just make sure that the string length is longer than the paper square by at least ½" (1.3cm) on either side.

3 Lay the first string right-side up on the diagonal. Pin it in place or use a small piece of double-sided tape between the fabric strip and the paper to keep it in place.

4 Place another string, right-side down on top of the first string. Sew the strips together with a ¼" (6mm) seam, sewing through all 3 layers.

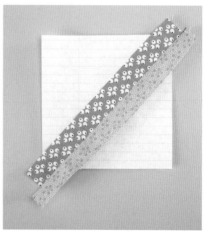

5 Press the second strip open.

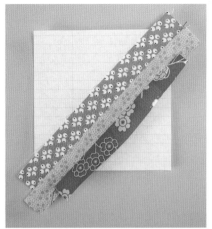

6 Lay another string (the third) right-side down on top of the second string. Sew the strips together with a ¼" (6mm) seam, sewing through all 3 layers again.

7 Press the third strip open.

8 Continue sewing strips and pressing them open until you cover the corner of the paper. Go back and work the left side of the block, laying strips on the other side of the first strip and working outward.

9 Trim the overlapping strips using the paper square as your guide.

10 Do not remove the paper from the back of the String block until you have finished sewing it into one of the sampler quilt blocks. This will prevent stretching and distortion due to exposed bias edges.

Binding

Binding your quilt is exciting because it means your quilt is almost complete!

There are many ways to bind and finish a quilt. My favorite way is to use straight-grain double-fold continuous binding with mitered corners.

I generally bind by machine because it's fast and provides a durable seam. For quilts that will get a lot of use or frequent washing, this is a good choice. Yes, the stitching will show along the back, but you can hide this by choosing a bobbin thread that's the same color as your backing.

Binding by hand is the traditional method of binding quilts, and it's extremely therapeutic. Sometimes it's nice to sit by the fire and bind while beneath your new quilt.

Instructions are given for both machine and hand binding. Try them both!

PREPARE THE BINDING STRIPS

You may make your binding strip width to your liking. I prefer using 2½" (6.4cm) strips cut on the straight-grain from selvage to selvage.

1 Cut the required number of 2½" (6.4cm) wide strips as needed according to the project directions.

2 Remove the selvages from all strips.

3 To join strips, place 2 strips right sides together and perpendicular to one another, aligning the raw edges. Draw a diagonal line on the top strip. Sew on the drawn line to make a continuous strip (Figure 1). Press seam allowances open.

4 Trim the excess, cutting ¼" (6mm) away from the sewn line. Press and trim any dog ears (Figure 2).

5 Continue adding strips end to end in this manner until you have one long, continuous strip.

6 Fold the strip in half lengthwise and press with wrong sides together (Figure 3).

Figure 1

Figure 2

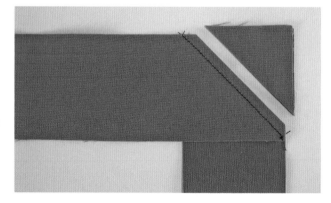

Figure 3

BINDING BY HAND

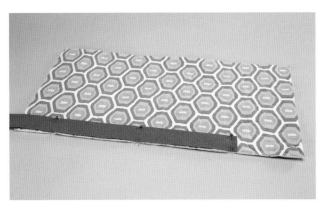

1 Pin the binding strip to the quilt top, aligning raw edges. Pin the binding strip along the entire length of that side of the quilt top.

¼" (6mm)

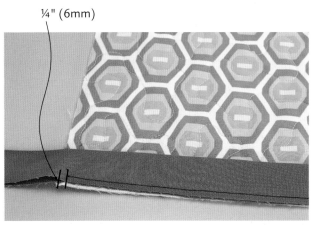

2 Using a ¼" (6mm) seam allowance, sew through all the layers, starting about 8" (20.3cm) from the end of the strip. Sew until you reach a corner, stopping ¼" (6mm) away from the corner. Lock stitch or backstitch and clip the threads.

3 Fold the binding strip to the right at a 90° angle, creating a diagonal crease in the fabric.

4 Hold the diagonal crease in place with one hand and use the other hand to bring the binding strip down and into alignment with the next edge of the quilt. Pin.

5 Sew along the next edge of the quilt through all the layers. Continue in this manner, sewing along each edge of the quilt and mitering at each corner until you have returned to the edge where you started. Stop sewing about 8" (20.3cm) before you reach the starting end of the binding and backstitch.

6 Lay the quilt on a flat surface. The starting end of the binding is already pinned to the quilt top (steps 1 and 2), and the finishing end has an unstitched tail. Lay the tail along the edge of the quilt, up to the point where it meets the starting end. Fold the finishing end tail back onto itself, then measure and mark 2½" (6.4cm) away from the fold on the tail. Cut the tail at the mark.

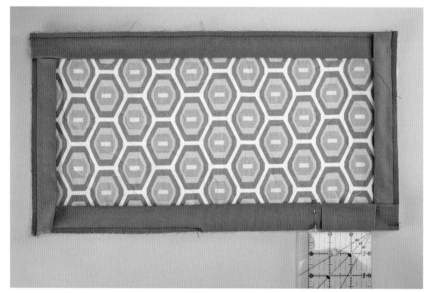

7 Remove the pins from the first strip and open both ends of the binding. Pin them right sides together at a 90° angle and mark the diagonal line.

8 Sew on the diagonal to join the starting end and finishing end together. Before stitching, check to make sure you haven't twisted the binding. Trim the excess, cutting ¼" (6mm) away from the sewn line. Press and trim any dog ears.

9 Finish sewing the binding strip to the quilt top, backstitching at the beginning and end.

The distance you measure back on the last strip is equal to the strip's width. In this case, we are using 2½" (6.4cm) wide binding strips, so we measure back 2½" (6.4cm). Adjust this measurement according to the cut width of your binding.

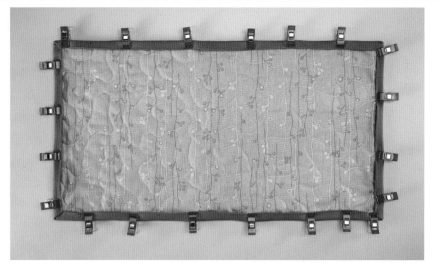

10 Turn the quilt over so the back is facing you. Flip the binding from the front over to the back of the quilt. Binding clips or hair barrettes are helpful to clip the binding into place.

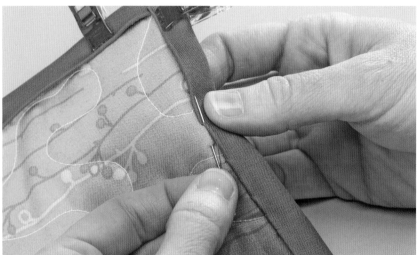

11 Hand-stitch the binding to the backing fabric, making sure to hide the stitching line.

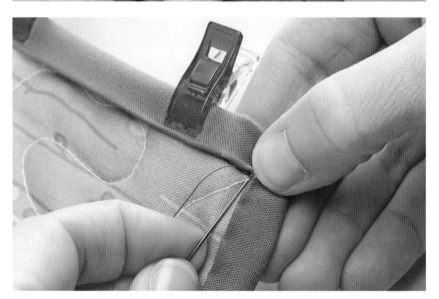

12 When you come to a corner, stitch all the way up to the ¼" (6mm) spot where you stopped before, then fold the binding to form miters before continuing to stitch the next side over into place. Use a few stitches to secure the fold in the mitered corner.

BINDING BY MACHINE

1 Pin the binding strip to the quilt back, aligning raw edges.

2 Follow the instructions for Binding By Hand steps 1–9.

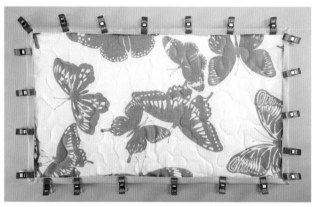

3 Turn the quilt over so the front is facing you. Flip the binding from the back over to the front of the quilt. Binding clips or hair barrettes are helpful to clip the binding into place.

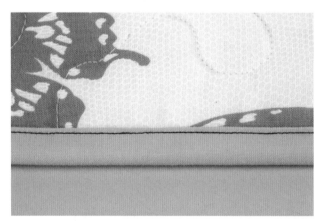

4 Topstitch ⅛″ (3mm) away from the edge of the binding to secure through all of the layers.

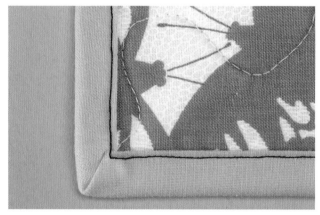

5 When you come to a corner, stitch until you are roughly 2″ (5.1cm) from the corner, then fold the next side over and into place. Stitch until you reach the point where the binding intersects. Stop with the needle down at the corner, then turn the quilt 90°. Continue sewing along the next edge. Continue along all 4 edges and backstitch once to complete.

ACKNOWLEDGMENTS

Thank you so much to my wonderful family for supporting me in writing this book.

To my husband, Matt: You are my sounding board. I could not have done this without your encouragement and support. And, of course, your willingness to pack up and take the kids to Grandma's for a weekend was an immense help.

To my three sons, T, G and M: You are always willing to help, be it removing paper from paper piecing, attending long-arm quilting appointments or jumping over preciously pieced blocks and quilt tops sprinkled on the floor.

To my parents: For your interest and encouragement in all my pursuits in life. To Mom, for testing for me and for being my biggest fan. To Dad, for offering to drive the GXQ delivery truck if I ever need one.

Thank you to my mom, Maureen, and friend, Cristin, for allowing me to put your quilts in this book as alternate colorway examples. Your quilts are beautiful!

ABOUT THE AUTHOR

AnneMarie Chany began quilting in 2006, teaching herself to thread a machine at the same time. It quickly turned into a passionate hobby and, in 2010, she started her quilt pattern company, Gen X Quilters (www.genxquilters.com).

Quilting marries creativity and precision, the perfect combination for her as a trained engineer. AnneMarie is the founder and former president of the Columbus Modern Quilt Guild (now the Columbus Modern Quilters). She teaches at local quilt shops and enjoys presenting lectures for guilds on modern quilting. She has appeared on *Quilting Arts TV*, and her designs are published in *Quiltmaker's 100 Blocks*, *Quiltmaker's Quilts from 100 Blocks*, *Fons & Porter's Easy Quilts*, *American Quilter Magazine*, *Generation Q Magazine* and *Modern Quilts Unlimited*. AnneMarie lives in Columbus, Ohio, with her husband and three sons.

Index

Sister Sampler Quilts. Copyright © 2015 by AnneMarie Chany. Manufactured in China. All rights reserved. No part of this book may be reproduced in any form or by any electronic or mechanical means including information storage and retrieval systems without permission in writing from the publisher, except by a reviewer who may quote brief passages in a review. Published by Fons & Porter Books, an imprint of F+W, a Content + eCommerce Company, 10151 Carver Rd, Ste. 200, Blue Ash, OH 45242. (800) 289-0963. First Edition.

a content + ecommerce company

www.fwcommunity.com

19   18   17   16   15   5   4   3   2   1

Distributed in Canada by Fraser Direct
100 Armstrong Avenue
Georgetown, ON, Canada L7G 5S4
Tel: (905) 877-4411

Distributed in the U.K. and Europe by F+W MEDIA INTERNATIONAL
Brunel House, Newton Abbot, Devon, TQ12 4PU, England
Tel: (+44) 1626 323200, Fax: (+44) 1626 323319
E-mail: postmaster@davidandcharles.co.uk

Distributed in Australia by Capricorn Link
P.O. Box 704, S. Windsor NSW, 2756 Australia
Tel: (02) 4560-6000, Fax: (02) 4577-5288
E-mail: books@capricornlink.com.au

Edited by Noel Rivera
Designed by Wendy Dunning
Production coordinated by Jennifer Bass
Beauty photography by Corrie Schaffeld
Step-by-step photography by Christine Polomsky
Illustrations by Hanna Firestone

SRN: T8811
ISBN: 978-1-4402-4503-9

Check out These other great quilting titles!

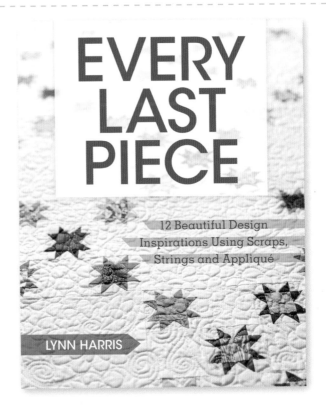

QUILT LOVELY
by Jen Kingwell

Quilt designer Jen Kingwell brings you fifteen amazing new quilt designs in *Quilt Lovely*. With nine gorgeous quilt projects that use a variety of techniques, including appliqué, hand sewing and hand quilting, and six fun pillow projects that can be expanded easily into quilts, there will be something for everyone to enjoy. Full-size paper patterns make template creation quick and simple, and an easy-to-navigate reference section provides advice on quilting basics and finishing.

EVERY LAST PIECE
by Lynn Harris

Learn to use fabric pieces of every size, from scraps to yardage, in *Every Last Piece*. Author Lynn Harris demonstrates numerous ways to maximize how you use fabric in quilts, including string-pieced blocks, mini star blocks, appliqué, sawtooth borders and more! Traditional designs are refreshed by giving them a scrappy look while other quilts offer minimalist charm when small scraps are used on broad backgrounds. The quilt gallery, as well as the projects themselves, will inspire you to design in ways you never imagined. Whether you're working on a gift, joining a quilt-a-long or heading to a fabric swap, you'll love using *Every Last Piece*!

FOR MORE, VISIT US AT WWW.FONSANDPORTER.COM!